Confession
And
Forgiveness

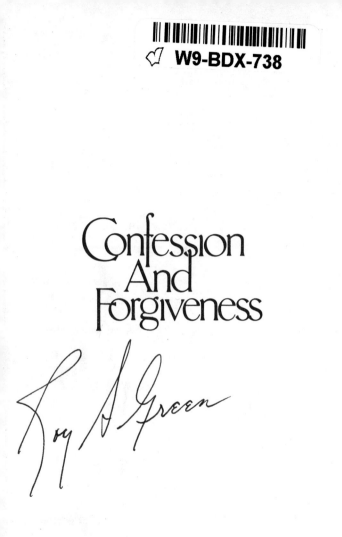

Roy S. Green

Books by Andrew Murray:

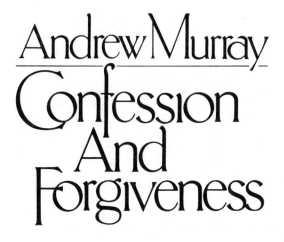

Andrew Murray
Confession And Forgiveness

ZONDERVAN
PUBLISHING HOUSE
OF THE ZONDERVAN CORPORATION | GRAND RAPIDS, MICHIGAN 49506

CONFESSION AND FORGIVENESS
Copyright © 1978 by The Zondervan Corporation
Grand Rapids, Michigan

Second printing   1979

Library of Congress Cataloging in Publication Data

Murray, Andrew Howson.
    Confession and forgiveness.

    Translation of Wees mij genadig.
    1. Bible.   O.T.   Psalms LI—Criticism,
interpretation, etc.   I.   Title.
BS14505lst.M8213   223'.2'077   78-12890
ISBN 0-310-29732-X

This book was first published in English under the title *Have Mercy Upon Me* by James Nisbet and Co., London, in 1896. It was translated from the Dutch by J. P. Lilley. Revised.

Printed in the United States of America

CONTENTS

IV. The Prayer for Forgiveness

V. The Prayer for Renewal

VI. The Sacrifice of Thanksgiving

TRANSLATOR'S NOTE

The Christian church has always taken a deep interest in the devotional exposition of certain portions of the Scriptures. There are some chapters of the Word of God that may be said to mark fresh epochs in the development of the spiritual life, and it has been found a most helpful practice for the ministers of the gospel to take them up in the worship of the congregation and make them verse by verse the theme of exhortation and appeal.

The fifty-first Psalm is widely acknowledged to be one of these cardinal portions of the Bible. Yet the number of detailed expositions of its meaning is comparatively very small. This lack has unquestionably arisen from the felt difficulty of doing anything like justice to its searching and humbling utterances. Much as the psalm has been used in preaching, ministers have felt so keenly the inadequacy of their efforts to set forth the fullness of its teaching that they have been glad to leave their lectures unpublished. No more diligent student of "the Treasury of David" ever lived than C. H. Spurgeon. Yet in writing of his study of the Psalms, he did not hesitate to use these words:

> In commenting upon some of them, I have been over-whelmed with awe, and said with Jacob, "How dreadful is this place! it is none other than the house of God." Especially was this the case with the Fifty-first. I postponed expounding it week after week, feeling more and more my inability for the work. Often I sat down to it, and rose up again without having penned a line. It is a bush burning with fire, yet not consumed; and out of it a voice seemed to cry to me: "Draw not nigh hither: put off thy shoes from off thy feet." The Psalm is very human, its cries and sobs are of one born of woman; but it is freighted with an inspiration all divine, as if the great Father were putting words into His child's mouth. Such a Psalm may be wept over, absorbed into the soul, and exhaled again in devotion; but, commented on—ah! where is he who having attempted it can do other than blush at his defeat?

It is not with a sense of having been able to succeed where others have failed that the honored minister of the Dutch Reformed Church at Wellington, South Africa, has been led to present the following exposition of this great psalm. A glance at the tender and beautiful preface that he wrote will show that he cherishes very different thoughts. It is only because he feels that this psalm contains a message that the present state of spiritual life in and around the church sorely needs, that he has been led to send forth this volume. The late Dr. Duncan of the New College, Edinburgh, used to tell his students that the one great heresy that afflicts the church and keeps back the conquest of the world for Christ is defective views of sin. It is because this psalm contains such an unreserved revelation of the soul's experience under the felt guilt, misery, and corruption entailed by sin, conjoined with an equally marvellous insight into the lovingkindness and tender mercy of "the God of all grace," that this fresh attempt to unfold its meaning has been made.

Therefore the whole exposition has been written with the utmost simplicity. What this generation needs is not

PREFACE

"THE GRACE OF GOD BE WITH YOU ALL."

Beloved in the Lord, receive in this prayer for blessing the greeting with which I offer you this book, with the assurance of my heartfelt longing and prayer for you all. It may at the same time serve as an intimation of the importance of the subject and the purpose for which I have been stirred up to write this volume.

The grace of God—a more glorious topic could not possibly be found. In that one word *grace* all that is wonderful and worthy of adoration in God and all that is glorious and desirable for man find their highest expression. The grace of God—what does it not include? The everlasting compassion that filled the heart of the Father until it at last overflowed in the gift of His beloved Son; the unsearchable richness and fullness of the grace that is seen in the love and the redemption of His Son; the blessed gifts and operations of the Spirit, of which everyone of the innumerable host of the redeemed is a witness and an example; all that is precious and blessed in the faith, the experience, or the hope of believers; and all that is inexpressible in the expectation of the eternal happiness that is beyond all understanding—all this is the glory of the grace of God. He who finds, knows, and possesses it has life and salvation.

In this work I have endeavored to present something of the glory of the grace of God, both in its first principles and in its higher operations, according to the teaching of this psalm. The misery from which grace redeems, the work that it does, the way in which it may be obtained, the blessing and the joy and the power it gives, this and very much more is presented in this psalm so simply, so intelligibly, and so strikingly, that I am assured the consideration of it cannot possibly be fruitless.

That it is also needed I know by experience. From many conversations in my pastoral counseling, it has become very plain to me that there are many, even well-meaning people, who have very defective, if not entirely wrong, ideas about the grace of God. Because of this they suffer inestimable loss. Wrong views about grace have an unhappy influence on the whole life. I do not desire that they should simply receive what *I* have to say to them about grace, but what I desire is that they should go with me to the Word of God and understand what *God* says about His grace, so that our thoughts about what grace is and does may entirely agree with the thoughts of God. Would that we could indeed endeavor to lay aside all merely human conceptions, all inherited ideas about grace, and with childlike submission ask what God Himself says of it. He who thus yields himself with humble prayer to be taught of God and is prepared to receive simply and without contradiction what God says will truly learn to understand grace. Amid all the various words of this psalm, that one word *grace* remains its predominating thought. The grace of God—may it be also for our souls the one topic that takes possession of us.

And what is my purpose and desire in emphasizing this

topic? It is that the grace of God may be with you and may be your portion and your joy.

I am afraid that some of you who read this book have not yet known the grace of God in truth, have not, indeed, found grace, because you have not yet sought it from the heart. You have long since heard of the grace of God, and yet it still remains strange to you. I hope to make clear to you the desirableness and your absolute need of the grace of God. In the light of God's grace, I would turn your attention to your sins, if by any means you may learn to deplore them with the penitent of this psalm. And with your eyes fixed on your sins, I would turn your hearts to think of the grace of God, if by any means you may learn to desire it, so that your earnest prayer may thus be: "Have mercy upon me, O God," I come to you with this prayer for blessing—The grace of God *be with you;* it is seeking you, it is for you, it will bless you, and be with you. You have need of it, and there is no hope or salvation for you if you do not have it. Allow it to come to you and be with you. Beloved friends who do not have this grace of God, with all earnestness I will cry to God and ask it from Him for you—The grace of God *be with you.* As your friend, I ask you to listen to me, while I proceed to expound the grace of God to you and in God's name endeavor to impress upon your heart that there is grace also for you.

I am quite sure that there are others among you who lift up the prayer of this psalm with all earnestness and yet do not taste the joy and the blessing that ought to follow the prayer. You still retain wrong ideas concerning the work that grace is to do, the way in which it manifests itself, and the conditions on which it may be expected and received. To all such I point out that there is a complete provision in the grace of God just for your needs as sinful and very wretched souls. I desire to make you see how suitable, how free, how simple, how certain, how mighty, and how completely within your reach the grace of God is. I would also have you know that your desires are certain to bring

15

you to faith, and your faith to a blessed experience. I would, above all, direct you to this prayer for blessing: "The grace of God be with you." You are praying for it, you are seeking it as if it were afar off. It is for you. It is near you. Simply receive it; only believe; allow grace to be with you. And for all who may read this volume I wish to make this prayer with my eye fixed on the God of all grace: "The grace of God be with you."

I pray and believe that there may nevertheless be among you many who already have learned to know in their own experience the blessed grace of God. For you not less than for others I have written these pages. This psalm, ordinarily regarded as chiefly intended for those who are penitent or who are seeking salvation, contains such glorious representations of all the rich blessing that the grace of God will implant in the soul, of the joy it gives, the power it exercises, the confession it draws out, the God-glorifying thanksgiving it enables the soul to express, that it will certainly help you also who believe, to understand what we may be by the grace of God. Brothers and sisters, come and see with me in this psalm the height to which grace exalts the penitent and hear the new song it puts on their lips in place of the prayer of the publican. Come and understand what your God will do for you. "Grace be with you." Experience it in its full power and in all its blessed operations, in all, especially, that it will be for you. Only give yourself unreservedly to it and do not remain content with anything less than all the riches it will give you.

"The grace of God be with you all." With this prayer I commend both you and this book to the Lord. May He graciously use it for blessing in the congregation where He has set me to work. May He also grant that where I labored in earlier days, or where the living voice can no longer be heard, it may be a blessing.

Your servant in the Lord,

ANDREW MURRAY

I

Introduction

To the chief Musician, A Psalm of David, when Nathan, the prophet came unto him, after he had gone in to Bathsheba.

The history of the Psalms is the history of the Church, and the history of every heart in which has burned the love of God. It is a history not fully revealed in this world, but one which is written in heaven. Surely it is holy ground. We cannot pray the Psalms without realising in a very special manner the communion of saints, the oneness of the Church militant and the Church triumphant. We cannot pray the Psalms without having our hearts opened, our affections enlarged, our thoughts drawn heavenward. He who can pray them best is nearest to God; knows most of the spirit of Christ; is ripest for heaven.

—J. J. S. PEROWNE

sounds until they learn to pronounce and know them for themselves. It is in this way that the Lord God deals with us in the psalms. He comes as the faithful One, bowing here more tenderly to our weakness. He Himself puts into our mouth the very words with which we may come to Him. He is aware that we do not know how to pray and what we should pray for; therefore He comes and tells us for what we ought to pray. And when we take these words of His into our mouth and continue to epxress them with the desire to understand them so that we may feel and pray as it is there expressed, then He gives us His blessing, and His Spirit makes the words living and powerful in our souls. Precious psalms, in which God's Holy Spirit Himself teaches us to pray.

The Book of Psalms will become yet more precious to you when you consider how the Lord God has given you the words that you may use when you pray. Has He sent us directions for prayer from heaven as if He had ordained them there for us? No, for then they would not be truly human, nor would they be adapted to our condition on earth. Rather, the Holy Spirit has taught us to speak in human language, with human feelings, from the heart. The Lord took people like us, sinners such as we are, in every possible condition of need and misery. He taught them by His Holy Spirit to utter these prayers and to commit them to writing; and now He offers them to us as a Prayer Book adapted to our need. Adapted to our need, I say, because they come from His Spirit and are therefore divine; and yet, they are just as genuinely human, because they come also from those who are our flesh and blood and were in everything like ourselves. That, too, is the reason why the Book of Psalms has been so precious to all sinners who are anxious about salvation, and has proved such a blessing to them. That is also the reason why it will become precious to you if you earnestly desire to seek after God. In other books of the Bible much is presented to you about sin and conversion and the conflict and blessedness of believers, but here you may see and hear these believers themselves. In the Book of Psalms you have the key of their inner chamber. There you may see them when they converse with God. There you hear how one confesses sin and entreats forgiveness and how another praises God for His grace and pours out his heart before Him. There you may kneel beside them and pray with them. Your heart will rejoice in their repentance and their faith.

What I am saying is that it is not only the inner chamber of believers that is open to you in the psalms; it is also the innermost recesses of their hearts. In solitude with God and in the light of His countenance, they lay all their misery naked before Him; and there you may see as in a mirror what wretchedness there must be in your own heart—wretchedness of which you still know so little. The inner conflict arising from the sense of guilt, as well as the joy of conversion and faith, is there presented to you in living and visible form. There you may see the struggles of a soul who is under the influence of God's grace. You will never learn to know sin aright, especially your own sin, until you have learned to agree with the deep confession of the suppliants of the psalms. And you will never learn to glory in God and rejoice in His grace so much as when you have learned to give praise and thanks with the poets of the psalms.

It is for this reason also that souls desirous of salvation have at all times deeply loved the psalms and that many of the most eminent of the Saints of God have declared that the psalms become more precious and more glorious to them the longer they use them, and that there is no means of grace more rich and stable than the right use of the psalms.

Yet why should I speak of men? Think of the Son of God. It is He who has taught us the use of the psalms and made them more precious to us. When in the heaviest stress of His conflict He Himself had to cry out, "My God, My God, why hast Thou forsaken Me?" was that not a word of the twenty-second Psalm written to meet His condition? And when He was dying and cried, "Father, into Thy hands I commend My spirit," was that not a word from another psalm? And if the man Christ Jesus had need of the words of the psalms to comfort and strengthen Himself in prayer to His Father, how much more must you and I have our hearts prepared by these divine prayers to draw near to God in a proper way.

The blessing arising from the use of these words, then, is great and sure—"The word is nigh thee, saith the Lord, in thy mouth and in thy heart." God has in His grace so adapted the Word to us that whenever anyone thoughtfully takes these words on his lips and uses them, a way is prepared for the Word to enter into his heart. Through the gateway of the mouth the Word comes into the heart. You will experience that the words of God are the living seed that germinates, sends out roots, springs upward, and bears fruit. Your heart is the soil; you have only to open it and you will experience that it is indeed the Word of God that works mightily in you who believe.

If you are one who is anxious to be saved, I invite you to meditate with me on the fifty-first Psalm. Let us learn to pray this psalm together. Let us ponder it, verse by verse, learning it by heart and receiving it into our spirit, as well as uttering it on our knees before God. For David this psalm was the way out of the depths of sin to the blessedness of forgiveness, to a rich experience of the grace of God. This psalm can also bring you and me into this blessing. It will do this for us if we use and follow it faithfully. Reader, for your own soul's sake, I entreat you, prepare yourself with all earnestness to learn by heart and to pray this psalm. The blessing it will bring you is inconceivably great.

2

PSALM 51

In the Psalter of David we find psalms of different kinds.
There are psalms of thanksgiving for praising and thank-
ing the Lord; there are psalms of instruction to teach us
one portion or another of divine truth; there are supplica-
tory psalms in which God's help is entreated in times of
distress or sorrow; and there are penitential psalms in
which, after confession of sin and guilt, prayer is made for
forgiveness and redemption.

The fifty-first is one of the seven penitential psalms,
and, indeed, the chief among them. To understand it
aright, we should especially note the situation David was
in when he wrote it. The superscription above the psalm
tells us that David had fallen very deeply into sin. He had
committed adultery with Bathsheba, the wife of Uriah.
But, more than that, he had tried to conceal his sin; and
when he did not succeed in doing that, he had Uriah put to
death. Even this was not the worst part of David's sin.
Had he but felt and confessed his sin, all might have been

well; but for nearly a year he remained unrepentant. It was only after the birth of his child, when God sent the prophet Nathan to him, that he came to a true sense of his sin. Nathan had drawn from him a sentence of condemnation against a rich man who had robbed a poor man of his only lamb—a pet lamb. It was only after the king had pronounced the sentence and Nathan had exclaimed, "Thou art the man," that he humbled himself and acknowledged, "I have sinned against the Lord."

The prophet had thereupon announced to him in the name of God: "The Lord has taken away thy sin. Thou shalt not die." This, however, was not enough for David. So amazed was he now at what he had done that he went to the Lord in deep self-abasement to confess his sin and entreat God to grant him by His Holy Spirit His divine grace for the forgiveness of sin and the renewal of his heart. It was at this time that the psalm was written, that is, as the superscription states, "when Nathan the prophet came unto him, after he had gone in to Bathsheba."

The reason, then, why I would have you learn to understand and take this psalm to your heart is that I think its lessons are so necessary and, indeed, indispensable. We are taught in our Catechism[1] that there are three elements in the spiritual life that we must know if we would live and die as saved souls. These three elements are: how great our sin and misery are, how we can be delivered from them, and how we should live in thankfulness to God for this deliverance. And nowhere do we find these great lessons concerning misery, deliverance, and thankfulness more clearly explained than in this psalm. Let us ask God to open our hearts to them and to imprint them deeply on our spirits.

The first lesson is this: *how terrible the might, the power, and wretchedness of sin are*. Think for a moment who David was: the man after God's own heart, "the man who was raised up on high, the anointed of the God of Jacob, and

---

[1]Heidelberg Catechism, Question and Answer 2.

the sweet psalmist of Israel" (2 Sam. 23:1). Think of the wonders God had done through him and had manifested toward him. In what deep trials he had been purified, how highly God had honored him, and how gloriously he had praised God; and yet see what became of him whenever God abandoned him for a moment and gave him over to the inclination of his own heart. Into what fearful sin has he fallen, and how long does he remain unrepentant? Nothing but the Word of God by the prophet can bring him to an awakening.

I fear that there are many among us who do not know their sins and have but imperfect ideas of them. The thought fills me with great sorrow, for, until they know their sins, they cannot really come to a confession of guilt or the experience of mercy. And unless they repent, they will die in their sin. When it is too late—in eternity—they will see what sin was. And that is the reason why I, as a servant of the Lord, come to you with this psalm. I would set before you the sin of David, and, like Nathan, say to you, "Thou art the man." I would show you, if indeed you do not yet know it, how corrupt the nature of man is; and how your heart, respectably as you may live in external things, is, nevertheless, the source of all sin and makes you capable of all sin, if God does not keep you; and especially I wish to show you how fearful is the power of sin to blind a person. You do not know your sin until the Spirit of God teaches you to know it. You do not know the real nature, the abominableness, and the curse of sin, until God makes it known to you; and therefore I urge you to come with me and listen to the prayer of David, a man of God. You will learn what you do not yet know of sin and its fearful misery.

And there you will further learn *what a glorious redemption is to be found in God*. Inadequate thoughts about sin and the confession of sin lead one to think little of mercy and the redeeming power of God. Something that is often considered self-evident and may be very easily taken for granted is that one should obtain forgiveness and enter into heaven; but in this psalm you will learn something different. You will see that great things must be done in you. David feels that he must be washed by God from his sin and that his transgressions must be wholly blotted out. He asks further that he may be entirely purified within and renewed in heart and that the Spirit of God may dwell in him always.

Come with me, then, and hear from David what must take place in you before you can be saved. You must be washed in Jesus' blood and be born again by His Spirit. This psalm will teach you that this glorious redemption is prepared for you and that, however sinful and helpless you may feel, you have access in prayer to a God who can and will work all of this in you. The prayer of David is indeed designed by the Spirit of God to teach you how you must come to God and what you may certainly expect to receive from God.

And then you will also learn *what a thankful life that of the redeemed soul is.* You will understand in this psalm how gloriously one who is partaker of the redemption of God feels himself knit to God. It becomes his one desire to praise and serve this God. It is a joy to him to make known to others what God has done for him, and that not as a burden laid on him, but as a work of love of which his heart has need and for which the grace of God gives the power. You will also understand how grace will sanctify not only the hidden life of the heart but also the outward life and conversation and walk, so that the redeemed soul may be known as one who through God has become an entirely new man to the glory of God. You will also especially see how all this is accomplished by grace in a sinner who has feelings like yours and is in the same misery as you are in. Yes, in this psalm you will see a man first confessing his sin in the deepest misery and anxiety, then receiving redemption through the working of the grace of God, and finally glorifying God as a redeemed and emancipated soul.

You must also follow this path if you desire to be saved.

I long for your salvation. Therefore I call you to join me in the study of this psalm, so that you may see how God saves a soul. Do not be afraid of the earnest words that I will use in talking to you about sin. The person who is not consciously a sinner and an ungodly soul, Christ will never save. Do not be afraid of the difficulty of the way of salvation; you will soon see how God will supply everything you have need of. Do not be afraid of the holiness and the life full of thanksgiving in which you must walk. You will see that God demands nothing that He does not first give and that the service to which He calls you is a blessed and joyful service of willing love, love that is awakened by His love shed abroad in your heart.

Gracious God, may we truly learn all this.

II

The Great Petition

1. *Have mercy upon me, O God, according to thy lovingkindness; according unto the multitude of thy tender mercies blot out my transgressions.*
2. *Wash me thoroughly from mine iniquity, and cleanse me from my sin.*

3

"Have mercy upon me, O God, according to thy lovingkindness" (v. 1a).

In this first cry of the penitent sinner lies the key of true prayer. In this cry for mercy we also find the key to the whole psalm. He who does not sincerely fall in with this petition will never understand the rest of the psalm. The prayer of David will be a sealed book for him.

We must not think that this petition is easily understood and self-evident. During the long period before David was brought to humiliation by the Spirit of God and came to know his sin, he could not of himself use this simple prayer; only the one who has been brought to an awakening by God Himself can be in a position to use this cry for mercy in prayer with his whole heart. And only he who prays this prayer from the heart can truly understand it. This must never be forgotten. David had learned to utter this prayer on his knees with a broken heart, in bitter sorrow for his sin. Much reading and much thinking may be necessary, but they are not enough for the right understanding of this prayer. It must be uttered *on one's knees,* with self-abasement, and *to God.* Then only can it become a blessing. Let us therefore look continually to God for His light and teaching, until by using it in prayer we have made this psalm our own.

"Have mercy upon me, O God." The true supplicant believes *that there is mercy with God.* God's mercy is the greatest wonder of His being. The omniscience of God is a wonder. The omnipotence of God is a wonder. God's spotless holiness is a wonder. None of these things can we understand. But the greatest wonder of all is *the mercy of God.* Here on earth we think but lightly of this and imagine that it cannot be otherwise; we are scarcely surprised at it. But it is not thus in heaven. There men are humbled at the thought of it and never cease to adore and thank God for His mercy. For there God is known as the holy One. It is known there that it is His honor to maintain His law and to manifest Himself against sin as a consuming fire. It is known there what sin is: the shameful rejection of the perfect One—of His law and His love. It is known there how entirely deserving man was of being rejected by God, and therefore it is that so much glory is seen in this mercy of God. That He should still have compassion for our fallen race; that He Himself should pay the ransom for our sin at the cost of the blood of His Son; that He should long after the ungodly, forgive them everything, and receive them to be His children—all this is so great that the angels cannot marvel sufficiently at such mercy. And it was because David had heard that there was such mercy with God that he drew near to Him with this prayer. We also must understand and believe that there is mercy with God.

Have mercy upon me, O God. The supplicant also feels *that he has need of mercy.* Mercy is something that is entirely undeserved, a gift to which we cannot lay the least claim. David feels that his sin is so shameful and makes him so guilty in the eyes of the holy God that it would be equitable if God should condemn him. Heaven would be bound to praise God if He vindicated His honor and His law in this way. Man has nothing he can boast of. If he has served God at an earlier period, that only makes his guilt the greater. It is not God alone who condemns him; he condemns himself. He feels that he is entirely deserving of the judgment of God; for his sin has shown how he had withdrawn from God, notwithstanding all the goodness of God to him. He feels that it will be a marvel of mercy if such a sinner is still thought worthy to be made a friend of God. The true suppliant feels that he has need of mercy and that nothing but free grace can be his hope.

Have mercy upon me, O God. The true suppliant desires also *that mercy may be shown to him.* He knows that there is mercy and he feels that he is one who has need of mercy; he is a fitting object of mercy. And yet this is not enough for him. He has need of more. He desires that God should show His mercy to him and make him aware that this mercy is also intended for him. He knows that the showing of mercy must be a personal action of God to the soul. That he knows there is great mercy with God can still bring him no rest. What he needs to give peace to his anxious heart is that he knows God is merciful *to him.* Be merciful *to me,* yes, *to me,* O God of mercy.

This longing is in full harmony with what God's Word teaches us on these points. The word speaks always of *finding* mercy, *obtaining* mercy, *receiving* mercy, *partaking* of mercy; and, looked at from the side of God as an action, it is called *having* mercy, *giving* mercy, *showing* mercy. Sin is a personal misdeed committed against the God with whom every one of us has to do. Conversion, likewise, is a personal coming to this God to receive redemption from Him in order that He may show mercy to the soul in taking away sin.

I am afraid that many are in great error on these points. They comfort themselves with the thought that God is merciful and have no idea that this of itself will avail them nothing. This mercy must be given to them by God and must be experienced in the soul. They forget that there is a work that mercy is to do for them and that he who is not partaker of it cannot enter heaven. They forget that God is the righteous One as well as merciful and that before His righteousness can liberate a single soul, His holy law must be fulfilled, and the sinner, everyone for himself, must have part in the righteousness of Christ and consequently in the acquittal of God. And thus with the word of mercy on his lips, many nevertheless go on to meet destruction; not because there is no mercy with God even for them, but because they have never had a part in the personal experience of the work of divine grace.

My fellow sinner, if you wish to learn to pray for mercy, remember these things: First of all, *there is mercy with God.* Let your soul be filled with the thought that with God there is mercy and that it is the highest joy of His heart to show mercy. Further, *you have need of mercy.* In the following verses of this psalm you will learn more fully how great your need is. Without mercy, you will be eternally and unspeakably wretched. But especially is this thought of the utmost importance, *that what you must have is a personal experience of this mercy as shown to you.* Something must take place between you and your God. You must *receive* mercy. Without this you cannot be content. God must do something for you. He must show you mercy. Let God's great mercy and your great misery be the two realities that cause you to utter this prayer all the more earnestly. "Have mercy upon me, O God, according to Thy loving kindness," until you have found mercy.

also know what we desire to have and whether we have also taken pains to know what He in his mercy has promised and can give.

And it is just at this point that many people err. Here, indeed, lies the reason that they pray for mercy so long and yet receive no answer. They have either very undefined or entirely wrong thoughts about what mercy can do. Some think that the first work of mercy is to comfort and enlighten the heart. It is not so. Later on in this psalm David prays for comfort and peace, but at the outset he prays for something entirely different. Others imagine that the work of mercy consists in the reformation of the heart and the life. This also is not the first element of blessing. Later on David asks for this also, but it does not stand in the first place. Others, again, suppose that they must ask for mercy and trust in it that it will bring them to heaven when they die, but believe that in this life we cannot know if we have mercy. David teaches us that, as with the previous idea, this is not what he desired first of all. What he wished to have, what the Spirit of God desires that we should be taught to desire as the first manifestation of mercy, is this: "According to the multitude of thy tender mercies blot out my transgressions."

Our transgressions must be blotted out by God Himself. It was in this conviction that David drew near to God. He feels that transgression must be blotted out; that he himself is not equal to this work; that mercy must do it for him. An expression used by Moses will make this clear to us. Moses says to God, "Yet now, if thou wilt forgive their sin—; and if not, *blot me . . . out of thy book which thou hast written*" (Exod. 32:32). Our sins also are written in God's book. The law of God takes account of every transgression we commit. In the great account book of heaven they stand against us as a record of our guilt. David knew that there could be no fellowship with the holy and righteous God so long as this old guilt was not abolished, completely blotted out. He knew that mercy could not convert or change the sinner or bring him to heaven, unless his guilt was first blotted out. The wrath of God must first be appeased. The old guilt of the past must first be removed. The sinner must have acquittal and the forgiveness of his sins. This is the first work of divine grace. Without this, God the holy Judge cannot receive the sinner into His friendship; and therefore he prays, "Have mercy upon me. . . . Blot out my transgressions."

There are many who suffer incalculable loss because they do not understand this. Perhaps you are among them. I will explain how this misunderstanding arises. It is because people remain unacquainted both with the holiness of God and with the dreadful character of sin. This is why many suppose that if only they have repentance, seek to live a better life, and pray to God, that God will on account of this great change receive them. It is not so, my friend. That you become changed is good. That you pray to be changed by the Spirit of God is still better. But this is not enough, simply because it does not clear the old guilt. The simple fact that you wish to have your guilt removed does not cancel it either with God or with man. What you must know before all else is how it stands with the guilt of your former life. Does it remain in God's book against your name? Or is it blotted out? Until one knows that it is blotted out, he can have no true peace.

So it is clear what we must ask for in the prayer "Have mercy upon me." The blotting out of guilt is indispensable. We cannot work this out by our repentance. God has promised to give it freely. His promise is "I, even I, am He that blotteth out thy transgressions for mine own sake, and will not remember thy sins" (Isa. 43:25).

This is what in the New Testament is called being "justified"; as, for example, in the parable of the publican. The publican prayed to God, "Be merciful to me," and he went down to his house justified. This was what grace did for him. This was the answer to his prayer. He went down to his house with the forgiveness of his sins. Like David, he could sing when he obtained this answer to his prayer: "Blessed is he whose transgression is forgiven, whose sin is by the external washings and sprinklings of the Old Testament that he was led to this prayer. Under the old covenant every priest had to wash himself as often as he had to draw near to God in Sacrifice. Every individual member of the congregation who had in any way come into contact with anything unclean, also had to be washed before he could mingle with the people. He knew that these washings had been intended by God to be symbolic representations of what must take place in the heart of man. They were a symbol of cleansing by the blood of Jesus Christ. The New Testament speaks of Jesus as He who has "washed us from our sins in his own blood" (Rev. 1:5). Of believers on earth it says, "Ye are washed" (1 Cor. 6:11); of the redeemed in heaven, they "have washed their robes, and made them white in the blood of the Lamb" (Rev. 7:14). With these expressions in mind, let us ponder this prayer: "Wash me thoroughly from mine iniquity."

What is meant by having to be washed *in the blood of Jesus?* The Word of God has taught us in what way the sprinkling of blood under the old covenant was a symbol of the cleansing from sin. Everyone who had sinned was worthy of death. But God gave permission for him to bring a lamb or another victim to die in his place. When the blood of that victim was shed, the punishment of death, which the man had deserved, was symbolically borne by another, and when the blood was sprinkled on the altar, it was as much as to say that this death, this shedding of blood, was accepted with God as valid, and that the sin of the one who had brought the sacrifice was washed away.

And thus the blood of Christ was shed as a propitiation for our sins. We are all under sentence of death. We have sinned and made ourselves guilty under the law of God. The law has uttered its curse against us as transgressors and can by no means withdraw its demands until they are fulfilled. God would not be a righteous God and a perfect Judge if He did not maintain the authority of His law and uphold its power, if He would simply welcome transgressors of His law into favor. Therefore no one can inherit heaven who is not pronounced clean by the law. And no one can possibly be pronounced clean who has not fulfilled its demands; and never has there been any man who of himself has been sufficient for this.

Therefore God in His mercy steps in with the gift of His Son. Christ has fulfilled the demands of the law in our place. He was our Representative, who appeared in our nature, to do in our stead all that was required of us. He was our Surety, who paid the price in our place. He was the Lord of the law, but was born *under law* to fulfill its demands. He honored it by a perfect obedience. By dying an accursed death He subjected Himself to its sentence in our behalf. He has borne our punishment. He has taken its curse upon Himself, and in doing so He has given what He had to demand from us. His blood, His soul, His life was poured out, and in the outpouring and the sprinkling of His blood lies the proof that atonement has been made.

And now it comes simply to this, that we should be *washed* in that blood. And what does this mean? Just as one cannot be bathed by having a stream of water flow past him, so it is with the blood of Christ. You must have a personal part in it. Your soul must come into contact with that holy blood in order to experience the power of it. Christ did not come, as many suppose, to abolish the claim of the law, but to fulfill it. The law has a claim on you, personally and individually, and will ask you if you have obtained part in the righteousness and atonement of the Lord Jesus. The law will inquire, Have *you* been sprinkled and washed with the blood of Christ? If you have been thus washed, then you are also acquitted, not because the law has no claim on you, but because you too are one for whom it sees that Jesus has fully met that claim. If you are not washed in that blood, then it avails you nothing that Jesus has died.

My fellow sinner, see now what is necessary. See now what must take place within you; else there is no hope for you. The Lord Jesus says, "If I wash thee not, thou hast no part with me" (John 13:8). With all your praying and seeking, with all your piety, you will not be saved unless the everlasting God works within you this spiritual wonder—unless you are washed in the blood of Christ. Do not, I beg you, despise the precious blood of Christ any longer, but hasten to God with the prayer of David: "Wash me thoroughly from mine iniquity."

Awakened soul, if you are perplexed about yourself and your sin, hear these glad tidings. Not only has the blood of Jesus been shed, but *God Himself is prepared to wash you in that blood.* God Himself will by the Holy Spirit bring your soul into an inner spiritual contact with that divine blood; will enable you to appropriate and experience the power of that blood. It is the work of God; He will do it. Only believe what the Word says to you. Believe that the blood of Jesus cleanses from all sin; believe that without any worthiness in yourself you can by the imputation of that blood be immediately freed from all your guilt. Believe that God is completely in earnest when He offers that blood to you, and in faith in Jesus' blood let your prayer become all the more urgent: "Wash me thoroughly from mine iniquity." Through faith in His blood we are "justified freely by His grace through the redemption that is in Christ Jesus" (Rom. 3:24).

6

"And cleanse me from my sin" (v. 2b).

It is easy to see that David's sin lies heavy on his soul. For the third time he pours out his desire before the Lord that His grace might liberate him from sin. Let it be understood that he does not speak of liberation from punishment. He does not speak even in the least degree of comfort in the restoration to God's favor. No, it is sin itself that is so terrible to him, and this he so desperately wants to have removed. That he felt deeply what sin was is seen especially in this, that every one of the three utterances he uses portrays sin in a distinct light. He felt it as a *transgression* of the law of God, a violation of the honor and authority of his King and Lord. He calls it *iniquity* according to its inner character, because it was the exact opposite of all that was good and holy, utterly unrighteous. And he confessed it as *sin*, a condition of perversity and misery. Concerning these transgressions of the law of God, he had prayed that they might be blotted out of God's book; concerning his iniquity, he desired that he might be washed from it; now, once again, in view of his sin, he prays for cleansing. In the earnestness of his soul, he makes known in the most significant way his desire for the redemption he expects from grace: "Cleanse me from my sin."

The word here translated "cleanse" is the same one that David found in Leviticus 13 and 14 in the laws concerning leprosy. It appears there ten times and is translated "to pronounce clean." We thus refer to these passages for the explanation. There we learn that whenever there was a fear that someone had the leprosy, he had to be brought to the priest. If he had leprosy, the priest pronounced him unclean. If he did not have this disease, however, the priest had to pronounce him clean. So also if a leper had been healed of leprosy, the priest had to pronounce him clean. After that, he might again return to the temple and enjoy all the privileges of the people of God. We see that in the New Testament, in the same way, the word *cleanse* is always used in regard to leprosy; and also that whenever anyone was cleansed by Jesus, he had still to go to the priest in order to be pronounced clean in the name of God.

From these and similar passages, it is clear that for cleansing two things were necessary, for purity, indeed, consisted of two elements. The one was that the sufferer should be cleansed from his leprosy. The other was that on the part of God he must be pronounced clean. In this psalm we find that in the purity that is expected from the grace of God these two elements also are found. In verse 7, "Purge me with hyssop, and I shall be clean" has reference especially to pronouncing clean, to acquittal from guilt. Later on, in verse 10, "Create in me a clean heart, O God" refers rather to the inner cleansing of the nature and the spirit.

Nevertheless, there is a distinction between the leprosy of the body and that of the soul. The leper must first be personally clean and then he is pronounced clean. The sinner, on the contrary, is first pronounced clean, and then becomes more and more partaker of the inward cleansing. The distinction, however, is not so marked as it appears. For the sinner is pronounced clean only by virtue of his union with the Lord Jesus. Jesus, the perfectly pure One, takes him up into His purity, becomes surety that this purity will be communicated to him. It is because he is clean in Jesus that he is pronounced clean and then he becomes all the more inwardly purified. And thus the two aspects of purity have one root, namely, the purity of Jesus.

And thus also the two are one. The same grace that pronounced clean also makes clean. The same repentance by which one desires acquittal also causes him to long for inward purity. And in this prayer "Cleanse me from my sin," derived from the word of the Lord concerning leprosy, David appears to have embraced both of these elements. What he later separates is here still united in this one supreme thought: "I would be free from sin; take away from me the sin that I have committed and the sin that is still hidden within me. Cleanse me from my sin."

It was the work of the priest to cleanse the leper. David desired to have this priestly work done by God Himself. He knew that although this cleansing is a hidden and spiritual work, it is nevertheless thoroughly real. He knew that no repentance, no conversion, no change of spirit or life, could cleanse him from sin. He knew that there is only one, the holy One, who is mightier than sin, who is in a position to cleanse him; and he knew that this God is the God of all grace, who will also do it. Therefore he prays, "Cleanse me from my sin."

What David found necessary we also have need of. He desired that the holy God would stretch out His hand from heaven and touch him and take away his sins from him. Let this also be your prayer; consider it: Sin is mine, it is upon me, it is in me. The purity that God gives may also be mine, on me, and in me. As surely as sin is mine, so also must the cleansing be mine. Otherwise, I cannot be redeemed. Yes, make David's prayer your own and make your own also that of the leper who cried, "Lord, if thou wilt, thou canst make me clean" (Matt. 8:2).

If you fail to do this with complete earnestness, go, contemplate your sin where David contemplated his. Read in God's Word how wretched the condition of the leper was (Lev. 13:45,46). Shut out from his fellow-men, from the temple and the service of God, he continually had to cry out, "Unclean, unclean!" for God had ordained leprosy as a symbol of sin. Pray that God may make you feel what a deadly and wretched disease consumes your soul; how you wander about, cast out from the presence of God and from fellowship with Him, and then pray, "Cleanse me from my sin."

And when you pray, Jesus will say also to you, "I will; be thou clean." The leper went out immediately, and was cleansed. Only believe in His power to cleanse, in His love that seeks you, in His grace sealed with His blood. You will then know also, once and for all, that the great deed of grace that you cannot now understand has taken place also in you.

Therefore—let me say it once again—let this prayer of David become your own. Like his sin, yours also is very great. As for him, so also for you, God is the only helper. Let your prayer, like his, be a cry from the whole heart: "Have mercy upon me; wash me; cleanse me from my sin."

III

The Confession

3. *For I acknowledge my transgressions: and my sin is ever before me.*
4. *Against thee, thee only, have I sinned, and done this evil in thy sight; that thou mightest be justified when thou speakest, and be clear when thou judgest.*
5. *Behold, I was shapen in iniquity; and in sin did my mother conceive me.*
6. *Behold, thou desirest truth in the inward parts; and in the hidden part thou shalt make me to know wisdom.*

him. He must confess that he has sinned, that sin has made him worthy of punishment, that God would be completely just to cast him away, that he is so entirely sinful that he can do nothing to make himself acceptable to God. As one who is guilty and utterly lost, he must submit to the sentence of God and confess that it would be a wonderful act of divine grace if he were to be received. It is only when man is brought to the point of thus confessing himself to be in truth and entirely a sinner that he will receive mercy. Then he stands in the presence of God in his true relationship; then he can honor and praise God in truth for His grace.

Nevertheless, it is just this that many who are seeking grace do not understand. They imagine that the source of a change of attitude in their hearts is God's allowing Himself to be persuaded to show them favor. They suppose that whenever they earnestly repent and learn to pray with much penitence and love and deep conviction, God will then manifest His grace toward them. And therefore they are always taking great pains to make themselves as pious and as earnest as they possibly can in the presence of God. They think that in this way they will receive light and comfort. No, my friend, this is not God's way. God desires nothing from you but that you should really acknowledge your sin and cast yourself down before Him as a guilty sinner. Then you will certainly and speedily receive His grace. It is as a transgressor, as one who is ungodly, that you are to come. To those who come this way, forgiveness and life will certainly be given.

The example of David also makes plain to us *the aversion of man to confess sin*. For a long time David was well aware that regarding Uriah he was guilty of violating the sixth commandment, and regarding Bathsheba, of violating the seventh commandment; but, as he acknowledges in Psalm 32, he endeavored to cover and to silence his sin. He knew that he had committed sin, but he did not know the sin in its enormity and heinousness; otherwise he would have at once humbled himself on account of it. This state of mind endured for almost a year, until he truly learned to know his sin. When, however, he could no longer restrain his convictions, he had no alternative but to pour them out and acknowledge them in the presence of God. And so it is today. Many who call themselves sinners are in some measure awakened to a sense of sin, but yet take pains to forget their sin. They have the intention of sinning no more and with this good resolution they come to God. They think they feel their sin with sufficient poignancy, and fear that it will make them too dispirited to ponder it deeply. Thus they keep themselves from really knowing their sin. The man who desires to receive grace must be willing to be aware of his sin and ponder it, and to become thoroughly acquainted with it. The more thoroughly he makes the bitter confession "I acknowledge my transgressions," the sooner will he be able to express the sincere prayer for mercy, and the sooner will he be prepared to receive grace. He will experience what David said after he had found that the suppression and covering of his sin brought him no rest: "I acknowledged my sin unto thee, and mine iniquity have I not hid. I said, I will confess my transgressions unto the Lord, and thou forgavest the iniquity of my sin" (Ps. 32:5).

This incident in the life of David also teaches us a lesson with respect to the knowledge of sin. It is this: *It is God Himself who must make our sin known to us.* It was only after the prophet Nathan had come to him in the name of God with the word of conviction "Thou art the man" that he cried out, "I have sinned." Man is by nature so entirely under the power of sin that he can hide it from himself even when he has committed it. This is one of the most dangerous manifestations of sin. It blinds the heart. It gives rise to pride and makes man unwilling to humble himself. It is the work of the Spirit of the grace of God to make the soul acknowledge sin. Often conscience can make one afraid of punishment, but this fear is the least element in the knowledge of sin. Sometimes trial or sickness or fear of death may make one tremble with the dread much that is shameful, so much that is heinous, that he becomes filled with this conviction. He goes forward continually bowed down under the thought of the great evil that he has done. Is not this what we expect from anyone who has done some extreme misdeed or other and then obtains an insight into its character? Suppose, for example, that someone has committed a murder and then repents for it; do we expect that he will speedily again go about laughing, or become very joyful? Surely not, especially if he is under a death sentence for his crime. So also, when a sinner becomes aware of the greatness of his sin, it becomes something he cannot forget, especially until he is certain he has forgiveness. He has sinned against God. He has made himself guilty against the law of God and the love of God. In the midst of all the occupations and distractions of the world, he testifies, "My sin is ever before me."

This is the great question of his life that he has to deal with. This is the one thought that occupies his mind: "I have sinned." And nothing can possibly yield him comfort until God has assured him, "Thy sin is forgiven thee." And although one may come to God with all sorts of fair words concerning the compassion of God, the soul still remains in this condition until God Himself takes away and blots out the sin. May we never at any time look upon sorrow for sin as something that is needless and may we never seek or seize a mere superficial comfort. No, a knowledge of sin is necessary, and it is the work of God to awaken this knowledge within us. Every soul must learn to say in the prayer for grace: "My sin is ever before me."

"My sin is ever before me." This cry ought also to remind us further of the *personal* character of a true sense of sin. A sure sign of those with whom the confession of sin is not deep is that they are always ready to say, "Yes, all men are truly sinners." It is as if the thought of the universality of sin makes the guilt of each person in particular less. At least this consideration tends to draw away the thoughts from the guilt of each individual person. From this thought one can go on to imagine that there are others who are still greater sinners for whom there is nevertheless grace. Why should there not then be grace also for me? This is the ordinary language of those who are not willing to think much of their own personal sin. They may have some knowledge, some ideas concerning the greatness of sin in general, but they do not say, "*My* sin is ever before me." This, however, is the language of the true penitent. He feels that he personally has to deal with God. He feels that he for himself alone has to deal with God, in death, in judgment, and in everlasting punishment, and that it is of small moment to him whether there are others along with him or not. He sees himself as one who is condemned and lost in the light of God's law and he has truly neither the time nor the desire to think of others. He cannot ask if the sins of others are greater than his own or not. He finds it sufficient to deal only with himself: "My sin is ever before me." He is quite in earnest with the confession "*My sin....*" While there are many who are doing everything to make it manifest that sin is not their own, he acknowledges it with all his heart. One person imagines that sin belongs to the devil; he has the guilt of it. Another fancies that guilt rests on the whole world and is dependent on circumstances. A third, not perhaps in words but in his heart, says that sin comes by imputation from God, who caused people to be born in this condition. But the true penitent cries, "*My* sin...!" Yes, sin is my own more than my property, or my house, my wife, or my children are. It is a part of me; no one can take it from me, or out of me, but God alone. It is a confession of dreadful earnestness: "My sin is ever before me."

Do you desire mercy? See here, then, what constitutes an element in the prayer for mercy. Do not turn away from the painful and humbling side of this confession. Consider no time or effort too much that you must spend to make your confession thorough and heartfelt. There will be much that you may desire to lay aside; but be assured that there is nothing that so much concerns you, there is nothing of so much importance to you, as your sin. In every thought God has of you, in every moment His holy eyes are fixed on you, this is the first and principal thing He sees in you: your sin. Is it not, then, of the utmost importance that you should see yourself as God sees you? In every prayer for grace that you make, this is the first point to which God looks: whether you indeed desire grace and long for it; that is, whether you truly abhor and condemn yourself as one who is entirely unclean, whether your sins are to you thoroughly and constantly wrong, and whether as a sinner you will know how to receive and value the redemption that is in Christ Jesus. Therefore may you learn to say with all earnestness, "My sin is ever before me." Without this there can be no true repentance, no sincere prayer for mercy, no living faith, no well-pleasing fellowship with God. We are destined for the knowledge and the enjoyment of the redemption of God here below and still more for blessedness and peace in heaven, where we will be praising and enjoying the free grace that has redeemed the ungodly.

I press these considerations upon you, because I know that there are many who deal too superficially with the confession of sins. They are willing enough to confess that they are sinners, for all men are in the same position. But unfortunately they know nothing of the tremendous seriousness of this confession. They do not utter it with shame; they do not utter it before God and upon their knees; they say it without really hungering for grace. May God redeem many of my readers from this insensibility and teach them to cry out in complete earnestness and with a contrite heart: "Have mercy upon me, O God . . . ; my sin is ever before me."

creatures will do what He has created them for? Is He not the God who in accordance with that right has given us His law, and is it not wholly reasonable that we should obey Him? And against this God you have sinned; that is, you have withheld obedience from Him. You have refused to do what He has commanded you. You have not hesitated to violate and to break His holy law. You have sinned against Him. You have exalted and chosen your will, unjust and perverse as it is, above His will. You have said that the counsel and the will of Satan is more attractive to you and has more influence with you than the will of God. As far as it was in your power, you have done your utmost to rob God of His glory. You have withstood Him. You have dishonored this great and infinite God. You, a poor worm of the dust, you have affronted and insulted the high and holy One before whom angels prostrate themselves. And as God is the Lawgiver and the Proprietor of the universe, He cannot endure sin. He must maintain His right in the universe. Every transgression of His law violates that right, and the terrible wrath of God is kindled to maintain that right. It is against this God that you have sinned. The moment one succeeds in beholding God in His greatness, does it not become self-evident that it is this that startles him and prompts him to cry, "Against thee, thee only, have I sinned." O what have I done? I have revolted against this God, the highest perfection. I have dared to provoke His wrath. This God, without whom I cannot live, I have made my enemy. Woe is me!

And this is not all. There yet remains one thought that makes all this still more bitter for the awakened soul. The God against whom I have sinned is the God of love. He has not only shown me His goodness in the thousand blessings of this life, but He is the God of love and the God of grace who has revealed His Son Jesus Christ in His eternal glory. And I have been such a child of hell that I have dared to sin against this God. I have despised His Son and turned my back on Him. There is in the confession an inexpressible bitterness for the soul who truly feels this: *"Against thee, thee only, have I sinned."*

It is this that makes sin so terrible. It is this that makes it wholly impossible for man to cancel his sin, for sin is an act of enmity against the holy God. And man is not in a position to recall this sin or to take it away. Every sin is an assault against the law and a violation of it, an inroad on its authority, and nothing that man is able to do can possibly cancel one single sin that has been committed. Sin has been committed against God. He has observed and marked it. It has assailed Him. He alone can say if He will forgive it, and He alone has the power to blot it out and annul it. Yes, the sin has been committed against God, and with God it must be accounted for. Once again, this is the terrible element of sin that is expressed in the confession "Against thee, thee only, have I sinned." And yet how little thought is given to it. How much awakened sinners concentrate their thoughts simply on the view that they have sinned against themselves and their own happiness, and how little on what ought to cause them the greatest concern, namely, the fact that they have sinned against God.

My reader, let this be the goal of all your effort. Make it, I urge you, a matter of much prayer. You have to deal with God. On the great day of judgment you will meet Him face to face. If you have not thoroughly learned to feel it, you will then experience to your everlasting horror what is meant by your having sinned against God. Even here it is grievous and painful to confess sin, but it is far better to be humbled here than condemned forever. And do not allow anything to draw you away from your endeavor to make this confession. There are thousands of so-called Christians who know nothing of this conviction of sin; but you may be certain that they will not be able to help you in that great day. Many will say to you that you must not make yourself too anxious about sin; but I feel bound to say to you that you have reason to be anxious about sin. You have sinned against God, and He is a consuming fire. Your sin is so great and the danger is so threatening that it that every single transgression of His law brings His curse on man. He does not make any inquiry about the excuse that man might make, but the sentence is inexorable: "The soul that sinneth, it shall die" (Ezek. 18:4). To every transgressor in the great day this word will go forth: "Depart from me, ye cursed, into everlasting fire" (Matt. 25:41). And the one who truly knows his sin admits that this sentence is not too heavy or too strict, is not more than he deserved; and acknowledges that God is perfectly entitled to deal with sin in this way and condemn him. The sinner has made himself worthy of this condemnation. However intolerable the judgment of God may be, he feels that it is not too severe; he makes confession that he has sinned against God, confirming the truth that God is righteous. This was David's confession. He could adduce nothing on which he could plead for any other sentence. If he were still to be received, it must be only on the basis of free, undeserved grace. He was, in truth, totally in earnest with his sense of guilt. He must have had a view of its detestable and abhorrent nature different from that of most men, in order to be able to speak thus, for he felt that the sentence of God was something terrible. In the anguish of soul that he had for a long time endured he had had some proof of how terrible a thing it is to be abandoned by God. Yet he acknowledges the righteousness of the sentence and yields himself to be laid hold of by it. That is surely something more than proceeds from man by nature. Such a sense of guilt and condemnation must surely have been wrought in him by the Spirit of God.

This becomes still more clear when we reflect further on the tendency of man to excuse himself. If David had wanted to make excuses, there was enough to which he might have appealed. Had he not served God from his youth on? Had he not for God's name and honor borne more than any other of God's servants? Would not the holy God Himself testify of him that he had walked with Him with a perfect heart? The Lord Himself had at a later period allowed it to be stated in His Word that He had strengthened Jerusalem "because David did that which was right in the eyes of the Lord, and turned not aside from anything that He had commanded him all the days of his life, save only in the matter of Uriah the Hittite" (1 Kings 15:5). And must this one sin of thoughtlessness be reckoned to him so severely? Would not an earthly prince know how to forgive a single transgression when committed by a faithful servant; and should not God the merciful and gracious One also forgive this sin of His own accord? There was no need for confession; God should not impute it to him. How often men speak and think in this way. They do not know the terrible reality of God's holiness and of His judgment on sin. They do not know that every single sin, though it be only one, is a violation of God's law, an injury to His honor, a proof of the enmity of the heart, and that it must be avenged. David bows himself before God, not merely because this must be done sometimes and because God is too strong for him, but because he had such a view of the authority of God that he approved of God's sentence. He saw how good it was that the law of God should be maintained, how needful it was that, though the whole world should perish, the glory of God and the honor of God should be established, and, under the power of that feeling, he makes confession of his sin as committed against God alone. In this way he sought to give honor to God and to acknowledge that He was justified in His speaking and clear in His judging.

Once again, therefore, I say that this is surely more than proceeds from man by nature. Such a sense of guilt and condemnation must surely have been wrought in him by the Spirit of God. The Lord has recorded this confession in His word so that we may see how it goes with one who is on the way of genuine repentance and conversion. What a different experience is this from the superficial confession of sin that most people are content to make. They confess, indeed, that they are sinners, but the sin is a weakness, an infirmity, a misfortune. They have to sympathize with the sinner, but of the honor of God they think with the confession of his inborn corruption. It is not simply this one sin that calls for punishment. He is aware that his whole nature is impure and that because of this, sin is never lacking, and he is a sinner who has need of grace. "Behold, I was shapen in iniquity, and in sin did my mother conceive me."

An acknowledgement of the inborn corruption of our nature is thus an element of the true confession of sin. How perverted must be the ideas of those who appeal to that fact to excuse their sin. There are many who do this even when they confess their sin. They think that since they are sinful by nature, the guilt of their sin is not so great. They cannot, indeed, be other than sinful. They were born so. They have their nature from God and cannot help that it is so sinful as it is. This kind of argument is a proof that they as yet know nothing of the real abominableness of sin. If they really knew it, they would be so deeply ashamed of their sinful nature and of the enmity toward God of which sin is the proof that it would humble them still more deeply to remember that they are one with their progenitors in sin. In view of the unity of the whole human race, they would see that God had put all of them to the test in Adam, and in this sense of shame they would be silent in the dust before God. The confession of this inborn corruption, then, and shame for it are both indispensable elements of a true confession of sin.

Only in this way can a person come to see himself as God sees him. Man looks continually at what is before his eyes, and when he does not commit an overt, sinful act, he does not think that his sinful nature is as much accursed as that of the open sinner. David ran the risk of being entangled in this error. But by the grace of God he learned to understand what he had been taught from his youth on: that even godly people have in the depths of their inner life the germs of all ungodliness and that grace alone preserves them from the development of these evil seeds. If this were truly felt, how would those who have been preserved from the ways of the ungodly in consequence of a Christian upbringing nevertheless know how to rank themselves in all sincerity with the greatest sinners. How would all of them subscribe to the representations of sin in God's Word and, in spite of a wide difference in the outward manifestation of sin, feel that they are on the same footing as other sinners in God's sight. For this reason also the confession of natural corruption is an indispensable element of the true confession of sin.

And only in this way is a person truly prepared as a penitent to desire and to receive the work of grace. If they are but single sins that I have committed, I can endeavor to make compensation for them. If I am inwardly and wholly corrupt, then every such endeavor is useless. Then every effort for good becomes stained with sin, and I have need of a free divine forgiveness. Then I feel that I have need, not only of forgiveness of sins, but also of renewal of the heart, as David united these two blessings in this psalm so closely with one another. As the confession of this inward and outward corruption becomes deeper, so the surrender to Jesus and His grace becomes more complete and unreserved, and grace itself more abundantly glorified.

It is, nevertheless, not simply the longing and the reception of grace that depends in large measure on this confession. There will also spring from it a clearer insight into the plan of divine grace and a cordial choice and enjoyment of it. When I see that my misery has its roots in my relationship to the first Adam, then I see how my new union with the second Adam redeems me completely from it. When I apprehend to some extent how the fall of Adam destroyed me, because I am born of him and receive his life, I learn to understand how the obedience of the second Adam restores me, because I become one with Him, am born of Him, and really obtain part in His life. The divine worth, the fitness, the all-sufficiency of the divine plan of redemption is made clear to me, and I know how to seek my salvation in daily fellowship with the love that flows from God. Thus from every point of view it is clear that the

12

**"Behold, thou desirest truth
in the inward parts" (v. 6a).**

The confession of his sin has taught David how to lay bare
its origin and root. From his birth on, his whole inner life
has been impure, and the thought of this leads him again
to think of God as the Searcher of the heart, before whose
eyes this inward corruption makes him worthy of rejection
even when it does not openly break forth in sinful deeds.
He feels that in his confession of sin and his effort toward
conversion, as well as in his hope in mercy, he must not
leave this out of view. The God with whom he has to do is a
God who desires truth in the inward parts. For us also it is
of great importance, in our prayer for mercy, not to over-
look this fact. It will teach us lessons of the greatest
importance.

God desires truth in the inward parts. *This thought
summons us to earnestness and godly fear in our sense of sin.* By
nature we run so much risk of dwelling more on the
outward manifestation of sin than on its hidden root and
power. Whenever, in consequence of their upbringing or
favorable circumstances, their outward life is religious

and unblamable, many flatter themselves with the thought that it is also well with their heart; at least that, although they have still many sins, the heart is not quite so bad as has been said. They do not regard themselves as being ungodly and enemies of God. When God's Word uses such expressions, it cannot refer to people such as they are. Did they but know how the Lord proves and searches the heart, they would think otherwise. The holy One sees the indwelling corruption of the heart. "There is none that doeth good, no, not one" (Ps. 53:3). The holy God requires truth in the inward parts. The service He receives must be completely true, in full agreement with His holy law. Love to God must fill the whole heart. If anything is lacking, we stand guilty and condemned before God. The fact that He cannot be content with less than perfect holiness is a terrible thought for the awakened soul. God desires truth in the inward parts.

This thought should keep many from the superficial conversion with which men so often allow themselves to be deceived. Whenever, on a sickbed, for example, there is a little anxiety about sin and questions about grace, the soul is at once comforted. Men are not aware that these feelings can easily be awakened and also very lightly laid to sleep again. One can desire the help of God without being prepared to abandon certain sins. The heart is deceitful above all things. Through the pious appearance of religion, people often deceive themselves. Oh that men might feel that God searches the very deepest recesses of the soul. This statement of David should be a word of heartbreaking power in order to be at the same time a word of healing and quickening.

Thou desirest truth in the inward parts. *This thought gives hope and comfort in the way of conversion.* Nothing less will God have from the awakened soul; nothing more will the grace of God require from the penitent. By facing truth, I learn to know myself as guilty and worthy of condemnation: "In me . . . dwells no good thing." How, then, can I arrive at truth in the inward parts? How can this thought give me comfort? In these ways: for him who knows himself as one that is lost by nature, the truth after which God seeks lies in nothing else than this, that he should present himself to God in truth as he really is. He who thus comes to God with the acknowledgment of his sin in his real condition comes in truth. This is the sincerity of which the Word of God speaks so much. There are many who imagine that sincerity before God consists in a great perfection and in a very cordial dedication of themselves to the service of God. For the anxious sinner it is not so. He is not yet so far on the way. With him this is the highest sincerity, that he should present himself to God with all his misery, that he should confess himself to be just what he is. He who confesses his sin certainly receives mercy. God desires truth in the inward parts. The one who is desirous of salvation and who rightly understands that requirement may rejoice deeply in it. When you appear before God, do not endeavor to present yourself to Him as one who is pious and to make yourself appear before Him at best with an animated religiosity. No, make confession of what you think and feel and do. Hide nothing from the Lord. Do not try to cover your sin. Acknowledge the whole truth about your condition of sin and misery. God desires truth in the inward parts and will not withhold His grace from you.

And when one has received mercy, there is still a glorious application of this statement of David. God desires truth in the inward parts. *This thought strengthens faith for glorious expectations.* One who has been endowed with grace has no conflict more bitter than that over the deceit and unfaithfulness of his heart. It feels to him that there is so much that is still not done in truth. In his faith, his love, his prayer, and his dedication to the service of God, he everywhere discovers that he is not yet capable of serving the Lord with his whole heart and in perfect truth as he desires. And many a time he is afraid that he will yet altogether fail. But then he finds in God's word this glorious promise: "I will direct their work in truth, and I will

13

**"And in the hidden part thou shalt make
me to know wisdom" (v. 6b).**

This statement appears to be a transition from the confession of sin to the prayer for redemption. God desires truth within. David is led to this thought by the confession of his inborn sin. It was not only his transgression but also his very nature that made him worthy of rejection by God. He cannot by nature stand before the holy Searcher of hearts, who desires truth in the very depths of the heart. But this thought leads him back again to God, who alone has the power to bestow truth in the inward parts.

The very fact that has brought him low, namely, that God cannot be content with less than truth, also lifts him up again. If the grace of God receives him, it will give him nothing less than grace. In the hidden parts God makes him to know wisdom. There is here in the heart of his prayer an expression of the hope that God will make known to him the way to be redeemed from sin; and that, deep and penetrating as the power of sin was, such also his knowledge of grace will be. He trusts that the spiritual insight into the way of redemption that he desires to walk in will be communicated to him by God Himself.

The whole psalm is indeed a proof that this is actually so. We have in this psalm the first clear explanation of the washings and the sprinkling of the blood of the temple service and the spiritual significance of the Old Testament sacrifices. The connection between the forgiveness of sins and the renewing of the heart is presented in David's prayer as clearly as almost anywhere else in the Old Testament. His hope was not in vain. "In the hidden part thou shall make me to know wisdom."

The anxious sinner who is seeking the way of grace may perhaps think that in this verse there is not so much as in other verses. Its instruction, however, is of the very highest value. In the prayer for grace this plea for wisdom is entirely indispensable.

It teaches us that *the true knowledge of the way of grace must be sought from God Himself.* He alone can make us know the hidden wisdom. The human knowledge of the way of grace that we obtain by the use of our understanding is not sufficient. Mark well: I do not say that this knowledge is not necessary. But this knowledge is not enough. This very book that I write is a proof that I consider this knowledge necessary. I am afraid that there is a great lack of an intelligent understanding of the way of grace. I am afraid that many have very imperfect conceptions of what grace is and how it redeems the sinner, of what the blotting out of transgressions and the washing away of unrighteousness and the cleansing of sin is, of what the terrible nature of sin is, and very much more that is taught in this glorious psalm. And I consider it of the utmost importance that one should have clear convictions concerning these points. For without clear knowledge faith cannot be clear and powerful and joyful. "Understandest thou what thou readest?" was Philip's first question to the Ethiopian. "Believest thou with all thine heart?" was the implied second question (Acts 8:30,37). Such an intelligent understanding of the way of grace is of great value.

But this is not enough. It is possible that one may have a well-nigh perfect knowledge of God's Word and yet be lost. And when we have clear insight into the way of the truth of God, we run just as much risk of being content with it. When one who was indifferent begins to be earnest and then obtains an insight into God's wonderful redemption, such knowledge sometimes gives him great joy. When he begins to gain a clear concept of the plan of redemption in Christ, of His atonement, of God's righteousness, and of the new birth, he sees such a suitability and glory in it all that he is filled with appreciation and gladness. But then he runs a great risk of resting in this. He feels a very great difference in himself compared with the time he was indifferent or ignorant. A great change has taken place in him, and yet it may be that he has not yet obtained an inward experiential spiritual knowledge of redemption. On this account, when an anxious soul is seeking to understand the way of grace in this psalm, it becomes a matter of very much importance that he should feel deeply his dependence on God; that at every verse and every word he should lift up the prayer "Lead me in Thy truth, and teach me: for Thou art the God of my salvation" and continually use, for example, the prayers of Psalms 25 and 119 to obtain the heavenly divine instruction of the Spirit in this hidden wisdom. If you are longing for salvation, remember that one may be occupied with divine truths and yet be lost after all. Perhaps someone thinks that such a statement is sufficient to make one altogether dispirited. It would indeed be so if we could not say in this prayer: "In the hidden part *thou shalt make me* to know wisdom." God gives the wisdom. This is our only security, and it is the only answer we can give to the question How do we know if we have a right spiritual knowledge of grace? The Lord can and will make you assured of this. Conversion is not a work that you must do and on which you can look back and say, "That is well done." No, the innermost essence of conversion and faith consists in coming *to God* in surrender *to God*, in receiving

IV

The Prayer for Forgiveness

7. *Purge me with hyssop, and I shall be clean: wash me, and I shall be whiter than snow.*
8. *Make me to hear joy and gladness; that the bones which thou hast broken may rejoice.*
9. *Hide thy face from my sins, and blot out all mine iniquities.*

14

"Purge me with hyssop, and I shall be clean" (v. 7a).

David has confessed his sins. Now follows the prayer for redemption, which he desires from grace. He desires before all else the forgiveness of his sins.

In order to understand this verse, we must look back to Numbers 19. There we find this word *purify* as many as seven times, and the ceremony of cleansing is described in complete detail. Whenever anyone had touched a dead body, he was considered unclean. Death was the punishment and the curse of sin, and for this reason every member of the people of Israel who had touched a dead body had to be considered unclean. He was then also no longer at liberty to come to the tabernacle, in order that he might thus show in an external way how contact with sin and death separates us from God. Only after he had been purified and washed could he again be declared clean. This purification also is described to us in that chapter. A red heifer had to be burned and its ashes put aside. If anyone had made himself unclean, the ashes had to be put into water, a bunch of hyssop had to be dipped in it, and the unclean person sprinkled with it. After he had washed himself with water, he would be clean once more. He must thus be purified with hyssop. In the Epistle to the Hebrews this ceremony is definitely mentioned as a type of purification by the blood of Jesus. We read there (9:13,14): "For if . . . the ashes of an heifer sprinkling the unclean sanctifieth to the purifying of the flesh; how much more shall the blood of Christ, who through the eternal Spirit offered himself without spot to God, cleanse your conscience from dead works to serve the living God?"

David knew that in this ceremony a spiritual purification was offered and he prayed that God might fulfill it in him. He felt that his sin had brought him under the power of death and that he was unprepared to serve the living God until he was first cleansed by God Himself. The light of the New Testament and especially this word from the Epistle to the Hebrews shows us that this purification can take place only by the blood of Christ. Let us reflect what David's prayer, illumined by other passages in the Word of God, can teach us.

It teaches us, first of all, *how indispensable this cleansing is.* Twice in Numbers 19 (vv. 13,20) it is written that whoever is unclean and will not purify himself shall be cut off from the congregation, because he has defiled the sanctuary of the Lord. God is a holy God; nothing that is stained with sin can stand before Him. Even if one had only touched a dead body, he might not enter the temple. By this external strictness under the old covenant the impossibility of any fellowship between God and sin is made absolutely clear. He who remains in impurity is condemned to death. If he would please God and draw near to God, he must allow himself to be purged with hyssop. God Himself had in a wonderful way prepared a sacrifice and water for cleansing, and there was no alternative but to be purified with hyssop or be cast out from the congregation of the Lord. In the New Testament it is still the same. God is the holy One. Sin cannot have fellowship with Him. God is the living God. Death may not draw near to Him; our sins are many, and we cannot blot them out. Even our apparently good works are but dead works. They bear in themselves the tokens of sin and of the death of the corrupt nature out of which they spring. He that is not yet purified in the way appointed by God, through the sacrifice commanded by God, shall be cut off from the congregation. Understand this, that nothing you can do, no change or reformation, can restore to you access to God. One thing is needful. You must be cleansed, and that by God Himself; otherwise you will not enter heaven. By all the terror inspired by the thought of being cast out forever, let this prayer of David become your own: "Purge me with hyssop, and I shall be clean."

David's prayer teaches us further *that this purifying is available.* The Spirit of God taught David to pray thus in harmony with what the types of the temple service taught. The New Testament says to us: "How much more shall the blood of Christ . . . purge your conscience from dead works to serve the living God?" (Heb. 9:14). Yes, it is the blood of Christ that can cleanse us. The red heifer was killed and burned, and its blood was sprinkled on the tabernacle. The water of purifying made from the ashes of this sacrifice could cleanse no one. Jesus is the perfect Sacrifice. He died for our sins. He has overcome the power of sin and death and canceled it. He has entered with His blood into the Most Holy Place. Be assured that you also may be purified and cleansed. Draw near to God with this humble prayer, that He would purge you, that He Himself would sprinkle you with this blood, and cause you to experience the power of it. He will do it. The blood of Jesus will cleanse you from all sin. If in faith, in the grace of Jesus, you seek to appropriate His blood, and on the ground of the word endeavor to hold fast the thought that *that* blood is also for you, the Spirit of God will give you the quiet assurance that God Himself has taken away all your unrighteousness from you. Go to the fountain of Jesus' blood; present yourself there to God, praying, watching, trusting. In answer to your faith it will surely be granted;

and you will know that you are clean.

> I hold my Saviour dear,
> For He makes me now appear,
> By His Word and Spirit clean
> From every stain of sin.

Yes, you will know that you are pure. Not that your heart is so holy that you cannot any more commit sin, but so purified by the blood that sin is no more reckoned to you and you yourself are no more burdened with it. And you are so purified by the Spirit, who is communicated with the blood, that you have a clean heart in which the law of God is written and in which it lives. Thus did Jesus speak to His disciples: "He that is washed needeth not save to wash his feet, but is clean every whit; and ye are clean" (John 13:10).

Let this prayer of David become your own: *"Purge me, and I shall be clean."* And the more earnestly you with your eye upon Jesus express that first phrase *"Purge me,"* the more powerfully will the Spirit of God also apply to you the second phrase *"I shall be clean."*

when he prays for a clean heart. But what he here speaks of is that entire freedom from guilt that everyone receives with the forgiveness of sins. When God forgives sins, He forgives at once and perfectly; and at that moment when God forgives sins, the soul is in His eyes and according to His holy law without a spot and entirely clean. As the Lord Jesus said to Peter: "He that is washed . . . is clean every whit" (John 13:10). Yes, "whiter than snow."

"Wash me, and I shall be whiter than snow." Would that every one of us might earnestly make this prayer his own. The arguments that should urge you to this step are great and strong. *Nothing less than this can keep you.* You may perhaps think that this prayer of David is too high. "I dare not ask for or expect so much. I will be content with less." My friend, you cannot be satisfied with less; with everything that is less you will be lost. We have said before that the law of God stands at the gate of heaven and guards the entrance to it. It lets no one in who is not *"whiter than snow."* That is the holiness of God and the perfection of the angels, and anything less clean and less holy is not admitted into heaven. If there is one single stain in you, the law will show it up. God will cast you out. The angels will cast you out. All heaven will cast you out. In the great day of judgment and wrath, when the justice of God will flash out against everything on which there is the least stain of sin, to consume it in the flame of fire, nothing that is not "whiter than snow" will stand before a holy God.

But you may be sure of this: *nothing less is offered to you.* If you had to purify yourselves to this extent, you might well despair. God Himself says, "For though thou wash thee with nitre, and take thee much soap, yet thine iniquity is marked before me" (Jer. 2:22). But instead of this, all that is necessary for your salvation God Himself has prepared. When God forgives, He forgives perfectly. "As far as the east is from the west, so far hath He removed our transgressions from us." The washing of the soul is God's work, an act of God's holy and all-prevailing grace. He is in a position to make it "whiter than snow." It is in the blood of Jesus that we are washed. The power of divine holiness, which is to be found in that precious atoning blood, has the power to make whiter than snow. In other words, the guilt-annulling atonement of Jesus Christ is perfect; His righteousness is perfect; His merit is infinite. If His righteousness is imputed to me, I obtain it perfect and entire. If I have part in the Lord Jesus, my Surety, then I have Him wholly and completely. Christ is not divided. Either I am in Him and have His full righteousness, or I am not in Him and have no part in it. When Jesus bore the curse for us, it was not imputed to Him and laid on Him according to the measure of His merit and worthiness, but *according to ours*. Now that we are endowed with grace along with Jesus before God, His righteousness is bestowed on us, not according to the measure of our merit, but *according to that of Jesus*. It was an act of the divine righteousness that Jesus came in our nature and took upon Himself our full curse. So also it is an act of the righteousness of God that we come to Him in Jesus to appropriate to ourselves the complete righteousness of Jesus. Jesus is treated as identified with us and, on this ground, as one on whom the curse must rest. He who believes is one with Jesus, is treated as such, is accepted in Him, and is "whiter than snow." God sees us in Christ. Our sins are entirely and completely forgiven; we are altogether acceptable to Him. He fulfills to us this promise: "Though your sins be as scarlet, they shall be as white as snow; though they be red like crimson, they shall be as wool" (Isa. 1:18). Therefore let everyone pray, "Wash me, and *I shall be whiter than snow.*" It is nothing less than this that God has offered to us.

Nothing less than this can bring you full peace. Yet how many are there who are seeking a ground of peace with God in their own activity and endeavors and experiences. But they cannot find stable, full peace, the peace that Jesus gives and that passes all understanding. Only when we can say by faith, "I shall be clean," "I shall be whiter than snow," do we know what is meant by saying, "Blessed is he whose transgression is forgiven, whose sin is covered" (Ps. 32:1) and what is meant by singing, "Bless the Lord, O my soul . . . who forgiveth all thine iniquities" (Ps. 103:1,3). Then a disquieted conscience obtains peace, full peace, even in view of God and of sin, in view of the law and the curse, in view of death and of judgment, because the blood of Jesus makes "whiter than snow." The soul rejoices with a joy that is "unspeakable and full of glory."

Nothing less than this must be your desire. What I ask you to do is to lay aside your own prayers and your own thoughts about what God is to do for you and to learn to pray as the Holy Spirit taught David: "Wash me, and I shall be whiter than snow." Take these words on your lips; lay them up in your heart; utter them continually before God in prayer; make them a continual aspiration. Then you will obtain a richer blessing than your prayers have perhaps brought you for years. These words will be to you a preparation for the gladness of that song of redemption that may be already sung here on earth: "Unto him that loveth us, and washed us from our sins in his own blood, and hath made us kings and priests unto God and his Father; to Him be the glory and dominion for ever and ever. Amen" (Rev. 1:5-6).

Receive this blessing now by faith. In Christ this grace is offered to you. Believe that through Him this goodness is prepared for you. Believe in Him, and you will not only ask with confidence but firmly believe that God is doing it: He washes me, and I am whiter than snow. Draw near to Him, then, and take the blessing out of His hand.

16

"Make me to hear joy and gladness; that the bones which thou hast broken may rejoice" (v. 8).

David does not long only for forgiveness. He desires still more. He also wants to have joy, gladness, and exultation. This is to him a part of the grace that he prays for. If this grace is to be full and free, he expects that it will, in truth, fill his heart with gladness.

Many who are eager for salvation do not understand this. They think that it is too great and too large a blessing to expect from God, that He should give deep joy to such unworthy ones. They would be content to be bowed down and depressed all their days if they could but cherish the humble hope of one day coming into heaven. They feel they are not worthy to ask for joy and gladness on earth as well, imagining that it is not fitting for them to expect it. They think that this is humility. Unfortunately, they somehow measure grace according to their own merits, and then it is not real grace any more.

David exemplifies how we are to know better the God with whom we have to do and how to cherish higher thoughts of the riches of grace. He knows that when God forgives, He forgives completely and when He receives anyone again, He receives him with His whole heart. The Lord does not desire that there should be any cloud between Him and the believing soul. He desires that a person know that he is restored completely to His favor, as completely as if he had never committed sin, and that he may now rejoice with confidence in the forgiving love of God. David knew this and therefore, though he had fallen amazingly low, when he asked for grace, he was not afraid to ask for complete restoration to the love of God and for the blessed experience of it. "Make me to hear joy and gladness; that the bones which thou hast broken may rejoice."

O that every penitent and anxious soul that uses this psalm may learn to understand that he is entitled to ask for nothing less than joy and gladness, and that it is proper for him to be content with nothing less than that. God desires this on the part of His people: "Rejoice in the Lord alway: and again I say, Rejoice" (Phil. 4:4). The Lord Jesus desires it also: "These things have I spoken unto you, that my joy might remain in you, and that your joy might be full" (John 15:11). The nature of grace, the glory of the reward, the love and beneficence of God, all entitle us to expect forgiveness to lead to joy.

And if we would understand what David's joy and gladness consists in, it is simply in receiving what he had prayed for: cleansing from his sins. Yes, it was from the forgiveness of his sins that he expected such gladness. It was always the sense of his sin that had grieved and pained him so terribly; and as long as he had no certitude concerning this blessing, he could have no peace. But if he could only know that God was reconciled to him, that his transgressions were blotted out of God's book, that he was washed whiter than snow, and thus restored to the favor of God, then his heart would be filled with joy and gladness. It was thus that he came to pray, "By the word of forgiveness spoken to my soul, cause me to hear joy and gladness."

How different is such an attitude from that of those who pray for a short time and then once again seek their joy in the world because they know nothing of the joy of God; or of those who pray for forgiveness and yet do not believe that this blessing can fill them with joy; or of those who seek the fountain of joy only in themselves, in some wonderful change of heart or holiness in their lives. My friends, learn from David that at the very moment you come in faith to the blood of Jesus to receive forgiveness, you may be filled with the joy of God: "Blessed is he whose transgression is forgiven, whose sin is covered" (Ps. 32:1). To the sinner Jesus says, "Be of good cheer; thy sins be forgiven thee" (Matt. 9:2).

But why is it, then, that so many never attain this gladness? It seems to me that this verse of our psalm points out a true reason. When David says, "That the bones *which thou hast broken* may rejoice," he reminds us how terrible his conviction of sin was. God had bruised him; that is, he felt that God was his enemy, that the wrath of God was on him, and that he could not withstand God or even stand before Him. The curse of God's law struck him down, and he lay bruised in the dust. The dreadful reality of sin and the terrible nature and certainty of God's wrath bruised him to such an extent that there was no healing for him, and now nothing can possibly comfort him, unless he is to receive complete forgiveness and complete restoration. If he were not certain of this, if there was to be the least doubt on this point, he could never find rest again. Was God's forgiveness a reality for him? He desired to be assured of this by hearing God's voice of joy and gladness.

It seems that exactly here is the reason why so many never come to the joy of God, and, in fact, never once earnestly long for it. They have never yet truly felt their sins. They cannot yet speak to God of "the bones which thou hast broken." They know that they are sinners; but the conviction is simply a matter of the understanding. The fear of the Lord never grips them. They have never

17

"Hide thy face from my sins" (v. 9a).

Here we have a new expression of what David desired the grace of God to do for him. He expects that God will hide His face from his sin and not see it any more. This also was one aim of the prayer, "Have mercy upon me, O God." This blessing is in entire agreement with what the Word of God teaches us. So long as our sins are not forgiven, they are represented as standing before the face of God in order to accuse us. God hears the accusation they make against us. He looks on them in all their heinousness as a transgression of His law, and they awake His wrath and displeasure. So it is said, *Thou hast set our iniquities before thee, our secret sins in the light of thy countenance"* (Ps. 90:8), and again, "For though thou wash thee with nitre, and take thee much soap, *yet thine iniquity is marked before me,* saith the Lord God" (Jer. 2:22). In bitter experience of his anxious soul this thought has become for David a terrible truth. He feels not only what he had confessed "My sin is *ever before me"* (v. 3), but, what was more terrible, that his sin was *ever before God* (v. 4). He saw his sins himself and he was terrified, but he also says that God saw them. Every sin that he had committed was there before the face of God. God grant that every one of you may feel this. Then perhaps you may learn to understand the glory of David's prayer. You will then feel that every sin, as soon as it is committed, goes to swell the list of your accusers before the face of God and that whenever a sin is once committed, it is no longer in your power: you can no more recall it or annul it, and no repentance or tears, no promise of new obedience, can cover it or take it away. Only an act of God, a wonderful act of God's free grace, can give you the blessed certainty that your sin is no more before God's face.

And what is this act of God? David describes it in this verse: "Hide thy face from my sin." To hide one's face from anything means not to see it; and this prayer of David is just according to what is said elsewhere; for example, "He hath not beheld iniquity in Jacob, neither hath he seen perverseness in Israel" (Num. 23:21). So also Hezekiah prays, "But thou hast in love to my soul delivered it from the pit of corruption; for thou hast cast all my sins behind Thy back" (Isa. 38:17). The prophet Micah says, "He will turn again, he will have compassion upon us. He will subdue our iniquities; and thou wilt cast all their sins into the depths of the sea" (Micah 7:19). Similarly, the Lord said to the prophet Jeremiah: "In those days, saith the Lord, the iniquity of Israel shall be sought for, and there shall be none, for I will pardon them whom I reserve" (Jer. 50:20). These words of Scripture help us understand what the forgiveness of God is. He casts our sins behind His back; He casts them into the depths of the sea, so that they can no more be found; He turns away His face from them, and sees them no more.

This is blessedness: to know that our sins are forgiven. Christ has canceled them. Our sins can never again accuse us. The face of God has turned away from our sins and is turned toward us in favor. God no longer sees our sin in wrath, but He looks upon us in mercy. This is nothing other than what the New Testament calls justification. When the sinner receives acquittal from his sins, he is indeed justified in the eyes of God. His former sins are no more to be found. God has hidden His face from them; and when the holy Judge no longer beholds them, then the acquitted soul may rejoice in the assurance of His favor and love.

At this point, however, someone may ask, How can it be that the omniscient and faithful God, who knows my sins, nevertheless shuts His eyes to them and takes no further cognizance of them? He is always the perfectly righteous One, and *that He should look upon sin and simply ignore it* is altogether impossible. But when God averts His eyes from your sins, hides His face from them, and casts them behind His back, He does this because through Jesus satisfaction for them has been found. When he receives from the great Surety the assurance that you belong to Him, that you have part in the annulling of guilt by His blood, then God has no longer to deal with your sins; they have been put away. And then it is just His righteousness that demands that He should no more remember your sins but hide His face from them. As long as your sins are before Him, God must behold them; but when they are imputed to Jesus, with the satisfaction of the Lord Jesus as your Surety imputed to you, God will not look upon them any more. They have been accounted for and put away.

Thus also we learn in what spirit you are to make this prayer of David your own: "Hide thy face from my sins." Look upon the Lord Jesus as He has borne your sins on the cross and taken away your guilt. Look upon the Lord Jesus with the complete atonement He has accomplished as offered to you by God. Look upon Him as really given for you by God so that you may receive Him with confidence and come to God in Him. Yes, look upon Him through whom myriads have received the declaration of acquittal and receive this acquittal also as your own. Look upon Him until your faith comes alive and you can say, "Jesus is also for me; God hides His face from my sins.

'Thou has cast all my sins behind thy back.'"

This is a matter of great concern—of intense importance. Your sins are all before the face of God. Justice cries out for vengeance. Day and night its cry ascends to God: "This sinner has provoked Thee; he is worthy of the curse; O holy God, hide not Thy face from his sins." And the law of God supports the cry of justice: "O holy God, they have transgressed Thy law; hide not Thy face from their sins." And woe to the sinner who must experience that. For this reason, pray to God: "Hide Thy face from my sin." Plead the promise of God and the blood of Jesus. Ask Jesus to become your intercessor. You will experience that God hears this prayer, that the blood of Jesus has great power, and that He is in a position to cover your sins and to take them away from before God.

forth. But before he proceeds to this, he once again utters the prayer "Blot out all mine iniquities." In this way he shows us that he was completely earnest about this matter. He knows that it is the root and the beginning of all the rest and that if there is no clear understanding between God and the sinner with respect to the forgiveness of sins, there can be no further question about a new life. And therefore I also will deal with this matter with all earnestness, with all definiteness, and with all sincerity. I want to ask some questions concerning this all-important matter.

Do you thoroughly understand what the forgiveness of sins—*the blotting out of iniquities*—is? Do not imagine that this question is needless. I know many earnest Christians who do not thoroughly understand this point. It will do us no harm once again to meditate on this—the foundation of our redemption. Do you understand that the blotting out of all his iniquities is *the first blessing* God desires to give the sinner who longs to be saved? Do you understand that God is prepared to give it at once, without further delay or waiting, to everyone who receives it trustfully? He offers it to us continually. Do you understand that he who simply from the heart receives the Savior with His blood receives also *by faith the blotting out of his sins?* Do you know also that by this faith with which he receives Jesus on God's word, he can certainly know that his sins are really blotted out of God's book, because the Holy Spirit, as the Spirit of faith, bears witness to him of this forgiveness? And do you understand that this blotting out is perfect and complete, and that because of it the soul appears before God *"whiter than snow,"* and one can look up to God as a God who is no longer angry with him? Do you understand all this, or is it still vague and uncertain to you? Do you feel, when we speak of these things, as though you are still groping in the dark? I beg you to come to a clear understanding of these points, for they involve your eternal salvation.

Again I ask, *Are you really seeking forgiveness and the blotting out of your iniquities?* I do not ask if you know that you need to be saved, if you are sometimes disquieted, if you sometimes pray, or if you perhaps pray every day, "Forgive us our sins." No, my friend, I ask you something more than this. I ask if in the presence of God, the Searcher of hearts, you can say that you are known to Him (for He has a book containing the names of all true seekers after Him) as one who really seeks forgiveness. Can God testify concerning you that you are hungering and thirsting for it? Can you say that day by day you are seeking and striving for this grace as something indispensable? Have you, to obtain this forgiveness, abandoned sin and willingly given up the world? And are you now with earnest prayer, even at unusual times (for true seeking will hardly limit itself to certain fixed hours), casting yourself before God to request it from Him, as the one blessing He has to give you? Are you really seeking it in the house of prayer, in God's Word, and in prayer in your own closet, as the one thing for which you are willing to count everything else but loss? It is worthy of being sought in this way. God desires that it should be thus sought; and only he who does so will obtain it.

Are you really seeking it in this way?

I have still another question. If you have not been seeking this blotting out of your iniquities until now, or if you have only begun desiring to seek it, this question does not concern you. But if you can say that you have been seeking it, then I ask you, Have you indeed found it? Are your sins forgiven? Do you know that, as surely and really as the guilt of your sin was upon you, so you are now really clean in God's sight, because He has blotted out all your iniquities? I know that many shrink from these questions, but it is for this very reason that I ask them. When David had prayed for mercy, he was not content with indefinite ideas about the goodness of God. He knew what God in His goodness desired to do for him. He expected Him to do something real for him. He prays for the blotting out of his iniquities with the expectation of obtaining an answer to that prayer and in the hope that then the joy and the power of a new life would be fulfilled in him, as he has so

V

The Prayer for Renewal

10. *Create in me a clean heart, O God; and renew a right spirit within me.*
11. *Cast me not away from thy presence; and take not thy holy spirit from me.*
12. *Restore unto me the joy of thy salvation; and uphold me with thy free spirit.*

His back, a person is entirely freed from the guilt that is resting on him, and thus he is judicially clean. That is to say, I have fulfilled the demands of the law; I have paid for my guilt, either by myself or by another as surety. Therefore, the law has naturally nothing more to demand from me. I stand before it guiltless and clean. The law always inquires only about what I have done and what I have been, not about what I still am or what I will do. Thus it may be that a judge on earth may acquit or pronounce someone innocent without implying that the heart of the acquitted person is clean or that he is beyond the possibility of again committing the very same sin. Similarly, the sinner is acquitted and pronounced clean from all the sins he has committed, without any implication that his heart is pure from the seeds of future sins. In fact, even though God knows that the heart is inwardly impure, as far as sinful disposition is concerned, the sinner is pronounced clean by the law as soon as all the demands of the law are fulfilled. The demands of the law have been fulfilled by the Savior, by His obedience and suffering, and therefore by accepting Jesus, one has the blessing of being pronounced clean in His blood. This, then, is the purity David spoke of in the first half of the psalm: the complete forgiveness of sins and being made "whiter than snow."

But this purity is not all that a person needs. There is a second cleansing that is the fruit and the consequence of the first. An earthly judge may acquit someone or pronounce him clean, though his heart still continues to cleave to his sins and he may go from the courtroom to commit them again. But when God does acquit the sinner and pronounce him clean simply and only for Jesus' sake, He begins also the work of inward purification. The very same grace that teaches him to pray for the first purity (the judicial cleansing from the acquittal of the law) teaches him also to desire the second purity (the inward cleansing that comes through the renewing of the Spirit); and therefore after David entreated, "Purge me, . . . and I shall be clean; wash me and I shall be whiter than snow," he prays here again, "Create in me [inwardly also] a clean heart, O God." The one is as indispensable as the other, or rather, the two are one. They are but two different ways by which the purity of Jesus comes to man. As soon as a person believes, the righteousness of Christ is wholly reckoned to him, and because of it he is immediately acceptable to God as one who is clean. The inward communication of the purity of Jesus to the soul takes place by degrees.

These two are one; but they should not be confused, as is too often done, to the detriment of many. The one cleanness is a root, the other is a fruit. The one follows after the other. Notice this carefully. David has first prayed for the one (vv. 8-9), and then he asks for the other. Never forget that the first, the cleansing by the blood of Christ must be given before you can receive the second and that only he who receives and accepts the first will have the power to obtain the second.

Let this be your prayer: "Have mercy upon me, O God; blot out all mine iniquities. Create in me a clean heart."

We understand now the place that this prayer occupies in this psalm. It has prepared us to feel the meaning and the power of the psalm all the better. May God teach us to offer this prayer with deep earnestness and with our whole heart.

The desire of the true suppliant must, above all things, go forth toward inward purity. David is not content with praying simply for the forgiveness of his transgressions. Because he felt that his whole nature was inwardly corrupt, he desires also to be inwardly purified. He is not content simply with acquittal from merited punishment. Unfortunately, many are content with this. No, he desires to be free also from the power and indwelling of sin. He desires to be holy and to stop commiting sin. He feels that only according to the measure of his holiness can he enjoy God, for, "Blessed are the pure in heart: for they shall see God." You who are seeking salvation, let nothing less than this be your desire.

You must also expect this clean heart. God the Creator is also God the Renewer. He can do this. As the work of the first creation was not completed at once, but step by step, so also will it be with the renewal. The holy God can accomplish this. He can make the unclean heart clean. It is not too hard for Him. This is what grace will do for you. You may certainly expect this blessing. When you pray for forgiveness, let it be but a step to the way to becoming holy. God is pure, God is holy, and no prayer will be more welcome to Him than that He should make you holy also. "Create in me a clean heart, O God."

20

"And renew a right spirit within me" (v. 10b).

When God creates a clean heart in a person, that person is born again. He is indeed a new creature. He has received the new life, the love of God.

It is nevertheless not enough that one should receive the new life. It must grow and be strengthened. A weak child is really a living human creature, and yet much has to be done for him to preserve and nourish and lead his life until he comes to the full stature of a mature person. A weak child can stand and run, but he must also become sturdy and grow in vitality.

And this is what David now prays for. He desires not only the new life with the clean heart but also a right spirit, or *a steadfast spirit.* That new life and that purity of heart are weak and tender at first. Very much has yet to be done in order to make them grow. The creation of God was not completed in one day; so also in the creation of a clean heart, time is needed before everything is finished and man enters his Sabbath, his divine rest. And because in the new creation, after God has implanted the first principle of life, man must willingly cooperate with God, so it is necessary that with a steadfast spirit he surrender himself to the Lord and His work. The beginning of the new creation does not depend on a steadfast spirit, but certainly the progress of it does. On this steadfastness depends also the degree of glory with which the new creation will be brought to completion.

Great loss may be incurred by separating these two prayers. They are intimately bound together. He who is content when he thinks he has received a new heart and does not then also strive with a steadfast spirit and with a resolute will to guard what he has received and does not endeavor to use and to increase what God has given him will soon have to mourn the loss of the joy of a clean heart. On the other hand, he who works and prays for this steadfast spirit will know the glory of purity of heart and the splendor of the new creation—the full certitude and power of his heavenly birth.

We must also pray that God will give us *a steadfast spirit*. Steadfast is the opposite of weak, uncertain, changeable, variable. What stands fast cannot be moved or overthrown. We must ask God for such a spirit. At the same time we must also observe in what ways God works to give this blessing.

This is the first thing that strikes us: *"Faith is a sure foundation."* He who stands on it will not be moved. Therefore we read of the righteous man: "His heart is established, he shall not be afraid" (Ps. 112:8), and therefore Peter uses the phrase "steadfast in your faith" (1 Peter 5:9) and Paul writes, "Continue in the faith grounded and settled, and be not moved away from the hope of the gospel." (Col 1:23). In Hebrew the word *believe* comes from a word that means "to be steadfast, to stand fast"; and the word *believe* just means "to continue steadfast." Since God Himself is a steadfast Rock, the foundation of all certitude and steadfastness, it must be by faith or holding fast to God that man can become steadfast. If you want to know what you ask of God when you pray for a steadfast spirit, this is the answer: the more you cleave to God and commit yourself to His Word and counsel, the more steadfast you will stand. And if you want to know how God will give you this steadfast spirit, this is the answer: by the Word. Let the Word of God be your food; assimilate and appropriate it; let it penetrate you wholly; let it be flesh and blood to your spirit. As you are guided by it, strive to think what God thinks, to will what God wills, in everything to be of the same mind that God is, to grow by His Word in you, to have it dwelling in you; then you will be established. In all your wishes and expectations, in all your desires and efforts, let what God has said be your rule, and a steadfast spirit will be renewed in you. If the Word of God is the rock of your confidence, you will be just as little moved as there is variableness or shadow of turning with God.

How did Abraham become strong in the faith in the midst of so many severe trials? The root of his steadfastness was the promise of God. And how did Caleb and Joshua stand so firm in the midst of the hundreds of thousands of Israel? They held firmly to the Word of God. And how was it so also with many other believers? The answer is simple: "They that trust in the LORD shall be as mount Zion, which cannot be removed, but abideth for ever" (Ps. 125:1). God, as revealed in his word, gives the spirit its steadfastness and strength.

And if you want to know further how a steadfast spirit will manifest itself, the answer is not difficult; it is *in the resoluteness of a steadfast will exercising dominion over the spirit and the walk*. The great defect of many believers, when they have the new heart, is their failure to set themselves with a steadfast and resolute choice to cast out sin and do the will of God. They do not actually obey the dictates of their conscience, the inward voice of the Spirit and the Word; they do not surrender themselves unreservedly to do the will of God as soon as they know it. It is fitting surely that every believer should have the holy purpose of doing the will of God without delay as soon as he knows it. On this point there should be no uncertainty, for there are many double-hearted souls who are unstable in all their ways. A divided heart makes them continually waver.

Remember that along with the new heart and along with a sense of sin and good desire, there must also be a steadfast spirit that will be resolute and will set itself positively to fulfill all the commands of God. This steadfast spirit must be made a matter of much prayer: "Renew a right [steadfast] spirit within me," and at the same time it must be a matter of much effort in fighting against sin. He who seeks it in prayer will certainly receive it and will be able to join in David's song of deliverance (Ps. 40:2):

> He took me from a fearful pit,
> And from the miry clay,
> And on a rock He set my feet,
> Establishing my way.

Do not forget it. In the prayer for grace and in the life of grace, the steadfast spirit must have a place. The young tree must not only be planted but must also become deeply rooted, otherwise it can bear no fruit. Let this therefore be your continual prayer: "Make my footsteps steadfast in Thy Word, and let not any iniquity have dominion over me." Observe that the fruit of steadfastness is freedom from sin's dominion over us.

mother is busy and the child is busy; but seeing his mother's face and knowing that she is near is the joy of the child. And should God not grant this privilege to those who receive from Him the name and the rights of children? Yes, He desires that in this world they should always live before His face, in the light of His eye, and with the assurance and experience of His love.

The value of this blessing may easily be understood. What a source of heavenly joy it must be to walk in the land of the living before the face of the Lord. What a joy to do all our work and to carry on our conflict as at the feet of our Father, knowing that He looks down on us with good pleasure. To be able to look up in every difficulty and in the midst of severe conflict to refresh ourselves with a glance at Him and to be encouraged by His divine friendship—what power this gives in conflict, what comfort in sorrow!

And do you ask, perhaps, how this blessing can be enjoyed? To this also the answer is not difficult. The child does not need to be always looking to its mother to enjoy being near her. The child is busy with his play or work, and yet immediately notices when his mother goes out. In the midst of all his working and playing, he always has the hidden sense of her nearness. And so it is with the true Christian. He can attain to being so closely knit to his God that he cannot miss His presence and in the midst of all the severe activities of his calling on earth, there may always remain in his soul the blessed feeling: "My God sees me, and I can look to Him." He works as under the eye of God. *Through this living and ever-active faith he beholds the invisible One, and abides in His light.* And just as one walks and works in the light without always thinking of the light, so there streams around him the spiritual experience of the presence of God as the light of his soul.

If you have been forgiven, it is of utmost importance for you to understand that this is a principal part of true spiritual experience. Do not forget that the aim God has in view in His grace and your redemption is to restore the broken bond of fellowship and love between Him and the sinner. True religion consists in this, that the soul should find its highest happiness in personal communion with God. Grace will give daily unbroken blessed fellowship between God and you. Hence you are taught in this prayer for grace that you must pray for this blessing and strive after it. Every day, and the whole day, you must endeavor to walk in the light of God's presence. And if you desire to know how one can get up to the point of so living that he can enjoy this blessing, this psalm gives you the answer.

In the first place, *walk in a sense of the forgiveness of sins.* Hold fast to the grace that has blotted out your guilt. Every day bring each new sin to the blood of Jesus, so that you may be washed from it anew. Seek every day a living conviction of the grace that sees you in the righteousness of Jesus as being "whiter than snow." Look up to the holy God, who for Jesus' sake pronounced you righteous and loves you. Without this it will be a severe and heavy conflict, indeed, an impossibility to walk in the light of God's presence. Remain steadfast in the faith that God is your God and your Father. Only by this faith can you continue in the enjoyment of the light and the love of God.

In the second place, *strive earnestly for purity and holiness of heart.* Let the ardor of your soul flame out mightily against all inward impurity and sin. Be careful in watching the indwelling unholiness of your disposition. Remember that you are bound to hate it, as God hates it. Rouse yourself to the thought that you are redeemed to be holy, as God is holy; and let this be your fervent and earnest prayer: "A clean heart, O my god, a clean heart!" Knowing that the work of the new creation is not complete at once, cry to God that He will accomplish His work in you. A redeemed soul who remains content with what he has, who does not earnestly desire to be holy, cannot walk in the light of God's presence. His worldly mindedness, his carnal and careless disposition, is a cloud that must separate him from God.

In the third place to walk in God's presence, *a steadfast*

22

"And take not thy holy spirit from me" (v. 11b).

David has sought a great blessing, a very gracious gift from God: that he may walk always before His presence and in the light of it. He has asked that his whole life on earth and his whole being may be sanctified and illumined by the consciousness that in everything he is living his life as in the immediate presence of God, under His eye, and in His favor. He has desired that his whole life on earth might be spent in converse with his God in heaven—a glorious life, which grace is prepared to bestow.

And yet there is something that is still higher and more glorious. That I may walk on earth in fellowship with God in heaven is indeed wonderful grace, but that the Most High should come down from heaven *to dwell in my heart* and consecrate it to be His temple—this surely is the full glory of what grace has destined for us. And it is this that David now longs for when he prays, "Take not thy holy spirit from me." He yearns for the conscious indwelling of the Holy Spirit.

Some may possibly imagine that this petition is not here

in the proper place. Nothing of grace is ever wrought in us, except by the Spirit. Even the first conviction of sin and the desire to pray for grace must come from Him. Must prayer for the Spirit, then, not *precede* all else? The answer to this question may be given in these considerations. The working of the Holy Spirit in a sinner who has been aroused to desire salvation is indeed indispensable, but it is hidden and unconscious. Such a person does not know that the anxiety arising from the conviction of sin and the earnest entreaties for mercy—and he does not know in the least degree whether they will be heard or not—are all the results of the Spirit's operations. On the other hand, when, at a later period, he does actually arrive at faith, he has the promise that he will know the Spirit; that the Spirit will not only work in him but will so establish His presence in him that he will both know and feel it. This, for example, is the promise held out to those who were awakened on the day of Pentecost, who had already, at the outset, experienced the operation of the Spirit: "Repent . . . and ye shall [thereafter] receive the gift of the Holy Ghost" (Acts 2:38); just as the Lord Jesus Himself said to His disciples after they had experienced the first workings of the Spirit: "If ye love me, keep my commandments; and I will pray the Father, and he shall give you another Comforter" (John 14:15-16). Thus the prayer of David here is not a petition for the first operations of the Spirit with a view to conversion. Such prayer is necessary and according to the will of God, and must be offered. But the petition here looks to that indwelling of the Spirit of God that is the privilege of the believer. He dwells in them, to teach them (John 16:13,14), to seal them, and give them the assurance of sonship (Rom. 8:15-16), to sanctify and prepare them for heaven (Rom. 8:11).

It is this lesson, therefore, that is taught the believer in this petition, namely, to expect not only a clean heart, a steadfast spirit, and the light of God's face, but *also* the indwelling of God's Spirit in the heart. Every believer may have, and ought to experience, this blessing. Without this, he does not live according to the will of God.

The prayer of David makes this clear: "Take not thy holy spirit from me." He speaks as one who has already received the Holy Spirit; his petition is that the Spirit may not be taken from him. He feels that, although his former great sin had been forgiven, he yet always runs the risk of grieving and quenching the Holy Spirit, so that he will then have to remain without the blessed experience of His work. He knows that, however truly the Holy Spirit is the Spirit of grace, who bears up the sinner with great compassion, He is still also the Holy Spirit who is sure to be driven away by the love of sin. He knows that through worldly mindedness and worldly anxiety, through lack of thoughtfulness and reverent attention to His workings, injury is done to the Spirit, and He is grieved, with the result that He withdraws His presence from us. The same result follows unfaithfulness in the use of the means of grace, such as the Word and prayer, with which His operations are bound up. It is with a sense of this great danger that David prays, "Take not thy holy spirit from me."

This petition is a part of the prayer for grace, for it is wholly due to the grace of God if the Holy Spirit is not taken away from believers. As often as injury is done to Him, He is dishonored and has reason to withdraw, so that, were He not really the Spirit of grace, He would certainly leave us. David hoped and entreated from the grace of God that the Spirit of God would not withdraw from him, even when he might have deserved the loss.

The lessons for the believer are especially these two.

First of all, the Holy Spirit will dwell in him. He who desires to be led in the way of grace by the hand of David must now know that if he desires to see preserved and confirmed the blessings on which his heart is set, namely, forgiveness, renewal, and restoration to the favor of God, if he would truly be all that grace would make him, then he must keep himself largely occupied with the promise of the Spirit and must keep his desires firmly fixed upon it. Let him search in the Word of God for all the promises concerning the operation of the Spirit. Let him know certainly that this gift is held out to him. Let him yield himself unreservedly to the Lord, to experience this glorious grace. Let him seek to live daily in the fellowship of the Spirit and he will experience that this is the highest blessing that is to be found on earth.

In the second place, this blessing must be a distinct element in the prayer for grace. The person who is desirious of salvation must feel that he is unworthy of this blessing and forfeits it at every turn. He must observe every day that it is a favor that God does not take away His Spirit. He must feel that according to the measure of the earnestness of his desire and prayer and faith shall his growing establishment in this blessing take place, and his communion with the Spirit become more conscious and effectual. And according to this measure also shall the preceding blessings, of which this is the seal and the crown, be more richly and gloriously given to him; while, on the other hand, the neglect of this prayer will result not only in the loss of this blessing, but also the suppression of the other blessings that may have previously been enjoyed. Let us therefore pray with all earnestness: "Do not take Thy Holy Spirit from me."

Let us give careful thought to this context. We have already seen that the first joy of one who has received grace depends on the knowledge of forgiveness. The sinner who has once been awakened to know his sin cannot possibly rejoice in God unless he knows God as One who has blotted out his sin. He knows that if this blessing has not been received by him, God is still his enemy and a consuming fire. Only when one has come to the Cross and received an interest in the atonement of Christ, can the thought of the holy God fill him with gladness. It is fellowship with the reconciling God that imparts joy.

In the same way, the continuance and growth of one's joy depends on deepening communion with God. The very first act of God in beginning this fellowship with the soul, namely, the forgiveness of sins, imparts gladness. The next work of God in the believer is sanctification, in which, through His work of restoration, He gives him a clean heart and a steadfast spirit, a life in the light of His countenance, and the indwelling of the Holy Spirit. This also gives joy. And just as one cannot experience his first gladness *without forgiveness,* neither can he experience continued joy *apart from a holy life.* As certainly as the guilt of the old sin robs one of all joy until he knows he is forgiven, so certainly will new contamination that is not confessed and put away fill the soul with darkness.

Both the one who desires to be saved and the one who has received grace, should reflect on this fact. The joy of forgiveness will not always remain unless it is confirmed as the joy of sanctification. In this experience many Christians have incurred heavy loss, through lack of carefulness or knowledge. When the first joy began to yield, they did not know what the reason was, or else they were unfaithful in not confessing the sad fact to God and ascribed the loss to God as a trial He had sent them. Had they only gone forward in the way of grace, had they but asked for grace, not only to be washed from guilt but also to be liberated from the dominion of sin, they would have found by experience that with the progressive work of grace in the soul God would give a progressive joy. It is the joy of God's *salvation* for which David prays. There is joy in God's salvation, and only in the measure that we yield ourselves to God, faithfully and wholly, we will enjoy it.

And thus this twofold joy is one, just as there is a twofold purity. It is sin that entails pain and misery. It is becoming free from sin that imparts light and gladness. It is one God who first rolls away the curse and the guilt of sin, in one moment, and then gradually makes the soul free from its power. The one who rejoices in forgiveness ought to know that there is a joy that is still sweeter, still deeper, still more glorious than this, when the emancipation from sin and fellowship with God that began with forgiveness are continued and are appropriated and confirmed in sanctification. The joy of forgiveness is but the beginning, the firstfruits, and is destined for the newly born child of God. It is the milk of the blessing. The joy of sanctification and of fellowship with God is for those that have grown up. It is the solid food, the ripe fruit of joy.

You who desire to be saved and have come this far with David in this psalm, let this petition sink deep into your heart. The joy and the blessedness of God are His perfect holiness. The joy of His children also is the joy of holiness. Without a clean heart and a holy walk the Christian cannot continuously experience joy. The life of sanctification is joy. The way of the blessed life, the clean heart, and the steadfast spirit, the life in God's presence under the leading of the Spirit, is sometimes represented as a burdensome and grievous way. God has made it a way of joy. Some sacrifice of the flesh may at the outset appear unwelcome and severe; but God has declared that he who will once and for all unreservedly yield himself to it will find in His service great reward and the joy of His salvation. It is only in the measure that the salvation of God is appropriated effectually and as an element of actual experience that joy can be tasted. Joy is not, as some have thought, a separate gift that can be received and enjoyed apart from further experience of God's salvation; no, it is the joy *of* when believers confess with distinctness and boldness what God has done for them and show by word and walk that it is because of His compassion that they can testify that God is faithful. In the presence of the world they must be a convincing proof of what grace can really effect. A candle is never lit to be hidden under a bushel, and so God desires that His people, the light of the world, let their light shine. All this David knew. He does not repudiate what God has joined together; and as sincerely as he had confessed his sin and entreated redemption, so also he prepares himself for the service of thanksgiving and love.

But he also knows his own weakness. He remembers how lightly his confidence before men may be esteemed. He had experienced what every believer can testify to: that the world and all that is of the world, even though it should assume the form only of a slight departure from God toward sin, must shut the mouth, or, if the testimony is given, must render it ineffectual. The feeling that he expresses in another psalm, "I have believed, therefore have I spoken" (Ps. 116:10), was the utterance of his own experience. He knew that unless he had the Spirit of faith he could not know how to speak aright. And with the consciousness that there was still in him so much of the fear of man as well as of sluggishness and unfaithfulness, it was necessary for him, before he passed to the promises of thanksgiving, to pour out a prayer for this gift of divine grace also: "Uphold me with thy free spirit."

David knew that he could count on it that the grace of God would give him this blessing also. Grace not only grants forgiveness of sins, renewal of heart, and sanctification of life, but is also prepared to put the soul in a position to praise God and confess His name in the midst of every duty to which it is called. This is a point that believers understand too imperfectly and reflect on too little. They feel that the forgiveness of sin is an act of mere grace on the part of God. They acknowledge perhaps that the sanctification of the life must also be wrought by grace. But they do not know that the free spirit, with its power, must also just as certainly be the gift of free grace. They are persuaded that the public cofession of the grace of God and the proclamation of His goodness to others are works that out of gratitude they owe the Lord, as the best they have to give. But they feel that they are not equal to this duty and continue often to lie helpless in their weakness and unfaithfulness, full of self-accusation and self-reproach. They are not aware that grace not only begins the work of redemption but also completes it; that with the same certitude as when they first prayed for forgiveness, they may also expect that God will put them in a position to fulfill their vows of thanksgiving. In the confidence that this was indeed the case David prayed, "Have mercy upon me. . . . Uphold me with thy free spirit" (or "a free spirit").

"A free spirit"—the phrase suggests important points. "Where the Spirit of the Lord is, there is liberty" (2 Cor. 3:17), freedom from all servitude, from all oppression, freedom especially from the fear and doubt that more than anything else weaken the soul. It is only in the life of the Spirit and the entire surrender of the heart to be filled by the Spirit of God that lasting freedom can be found. It is always only freedom before God that makes us free also in relation to man. And for this full confidence before God it is indispensable that we turn to Him often, hold much fellowship with Him, and be conscious of maintaining an unreserved surrender to His will and service. He who has thus assured his heart before God will never need to fear any man. The continued unclouded consciousness of God's friendship, nourished in hidden, intimate fellowship with Him, will make the soul free from the dominion of the fear of man, and, besides, put it in a position to testify of the praise of God.

Believer, pray for a free spirit. Grace will certainly give it to you. You hinder grace in its work if you remain without this blessing. You allow yourself to be contented with half of what the grace of God is prepared to do for you. You defraud grace of the honor due it if you continue

VI

The Sacrifice of Thanksgiving

13. *Then will I teach transgressors thy ways; and sinners shall be converted unto thee.*
14. *Deliver me from bloodguiltiness, O God, thou God of my salvation; and my tongue shall sing aloud of thy righteousness.*
15. *O Lord, open thou my lips; and my mouth shall show forth thy praise.*
16. *For thou desirest not sacrifice, else would I give it; thou delightest not in burnt offering.*
17. *The sacrifices of God are a broken spirit: a broken and a contrite heart, O God, thou wilt not despise.*
18. *Do good in thy good pleasure unto Zion: build Thou the walls of Jerusalem.*
19. *Then shalt thou be pleased with the sacrifices of righteousness, with burnt offering, and whole burnt offering: then shall they offer bullocks upon thine altar.*

nifies Him and makes known the great things He has done for him.

No man lights a candle and puts it under a bushel; much less would the Most High God do so. To all whom He translates out of the kingdom of darkness He says, "Ye are the light of the world. . . . Let your light . . . shine" (Matt. 5:14,16). If with David you have offered this prayer for grace and have hope that there is grace for you, fix your attention carefully on what the Holy Spirit would teach you from it. The design of grace is to make you a witness for the love of God and at the same time a monument of His wonderful goodness. Surrender yourself to this aim and plan of God and say in His strength, when you pray for grace, "Then will I teach transgressors thy ways."

Do not imagine, however, that God requires this of you as a debt that you must pay to Him in return for your redemption. No, if you yield yourself to this work in the strength of grace, it will be your greatest joy to say, "Then will I teach transgressors thy ways." When you think of the abyss out of which you have been rescued and the glorious salvation that has become yours, of the deep misery in which others still lie overwhelmed and how God's precious grace is also for them, mighty and ready to redeem them as it has redeemed you, your heart will be filled with compassion for sinners and you will count it a blessing that you may exercise the privilege of speaking of Jesus to others. When you reflect what the love of Jesus has done for you and how much you have to thank Him for, this love will inspire you; and as often as you pray anew, "O God, have mercy on me; then will I teach transgressors Thy way," the desire will be awakened in you that others also, who are still far from the precious Savior, and strangers to Him, may learn to know Him as you also now know Him. You always have the assurance that then only will they be truly happy and, what is more, then also they will glorify the Lord. For you feel more than you are able to express in words how truly worthy He is to be known and glorified. The mere thought that this and that "transgressor" might be awakened to life, that this and that worldly person might be changed into an example of one changed by the grace of God—and this through your prayer and your teaching—this, I say, is sufficient to make your heart burst with joy. And this will not appear impossible to you, if you look to Him who has shown you favor and to His love for sinners—love that will condescend to make use also of your service.

But I know well what other thoughts will trouble you. You will also think of your own unfitness for this task and you will feel that you do not know how you will ever be in a position to teach transgressors God's ways. The joy and the gladness of redemption are well-nigh taken away from you through dread of having to face this great and heavy duty. Observe, then, that this promise emerges in a prayer—a prayer for grace. David only says that if God shows him favor, restores to him the joy of His salvation, and grants him the upholding of a free spirit, he will then teach transgressors His ways. *The Lord does not require of you more than what He Himself will enable you to perform.* Do not forget that to one who has had his heart filled with grace it is a source of pleasure, a joy, to make others acquainted with Jesus. Acknowledge that the reason why it seems so unpleasant to speak of Jesus is nothing but the fact that we ourselves are content with so little of the grace of God that we do not yield ourselves to be wholly filled with it. Let the fear and the unpleasantness that you feel convince you that you do not yet have as much grace as God is prepared to give. God desires to give to every soul so much blessing that his mouth will overflow because his heart is full, that he will not be able to remain silent, that love to Jesus and to souls will constrain him to speak. Go therefore to God again, and still more earnestly, with a prayer for the full joy of the forgiveness of sins and for the full indwelling of the Spirit: then *you also will* teach transgressors His ways. Set this duty constantly before you. It is this that God desires from those who have been enriched with grace. It is this service that grace will enable you to render. It is by this that you will discover the true joy and the full power of grace.

Perhaps you ask where and when, to whom and how, you are to teach God's ways. All this the Lord Himself will make known to you. The compelling power of love itself will teach you this. Love will seek and create opportunities. Are you lying on a sickbed? You have still a grand opportunity for teaching others. Is your circle of acquaintances narrow and limited? In your own house there may be some to whom the ways of God are unknown. Are you simple and ignorant? It is the words of such that often find the fullest entrance into the hearts of others. The world is full of transgressors, and the heart of Jesus is full of love. If you have really tasted His love, you must admit that there can be no work so glorious as to be the messenger and servant of this love to redeem souls that are facing perdition. And if, besides this, you know that this grace that has made you alive from the dead is also able to open your mouth and thereby give this wonderful blessing to others, this also is worked out in you for a worthy end. Remember that every one who has been endowed with grace is called to the work of teaching transgressors God's ways and will receive strength to do it with a willing and joyful heart.

26

"And sinners shall be converted unto thee" (v. 13b).

We have seen that David had sinned deeply and still felt his fall keenly. If there was anyone who had reason to stand ashamed, never to trust himself, and to be silent, it was David. If there was anyone who had reason to say that he did not know to what plight he might yet come, it was David. And if there was anyone who had reason to say that by his unfaithfulness and the reproach he had brought on his earlier confession he had no right to speak and no one was under an obligation to listen to him, and that on account of his sin his words would be stripped of all force, it was David. How exalted he had been in other days, and how deeply had he fallen now. Nevertheless, in this psalm David is in touch with God and His grace; in his prayer he already anticipates the glory of God's grace. He feels that the grace of God is more powerful than his sin and that as grace could take away his sin before God, so also it could prevent his sin from barring his access to men. He feels that if God by His grace had redeemed him, the chief of sinners, and had shown His great goodness to him, He would also be prepared to make use of him as a blessing to others. Therefore he not only promises, "I will teach transgressors thy ways," but he also believes that God will certainly bless his work: "Sinners shall be converted unto thee." He trusts in grace for others, even as for himself. The grace that has blessed him will make him a blessing. "I will teach transgressors thy ways; *and sinners shall be converted unto thee.*"

It may easily be conceived that there is great power in the confidence that there will be blessing on our work. With what spirit and pleasure one will work in the sure prospect that God will give the increase. And the great question for us must be this: How shall we maintain this confidence? Let us consider carefully on what foundation it rests.

Remember, first of all, that conversion occurs by *the use of means:* "I will *teach* transgressors . . . sinners shall be converted." It is not enough to mourn over the poor unbelieving world. It is not even enough to pray for the conversion of sinners. Something more is necessary. They must be taught. And this teaching must not simply be dispensed on the Lord's Day, or be handed over to the preachers of the gospel; every believer must within his own circle faithfully perform and carry out the task promised in verse 13. After the prayer "Have mercy upon me" the promise must follow: "I will teach"; God is faithful to grant conversion. What a marvelous change would take place in a congregation if, with all wisdom and perseverance, unanimously and continuously, every believer were a witness for God. Faithful witnessing would give one courage to expect that sinners would be converted to God.

Observe, further, *in what spirit* the means are to be used. David says that, as one who had been pardoned, who had received the forgiveness of God and the joy of His salvation, he will teach transgressors. This is his chief concern. Alas! how many preachers, Sunday school teachers, Christian elders, and friends are there in whose teaching there is no power and who never see the fulfillment of the hope that sinners will be converted. It is not that they are not zealous or that they do not teach the truth, even the truths of this psalm, but they do not speak in the living experience of this grace. They teach in the power of a knowledge of the truths of Scripture or in the power of an earlier spiritual experience. But this is not enough. If you desire to see the teaching and conversion of sinners, there must be in you a living and effective experience of the grace of God. The blotting out of your guilt in a tender and daily trust in Jesus must be the joy of your soul. A progressive sanctification must be evident in your life through the purifying of your heart and the renewing of a steadfast spirit. With the prayer "Take not thy holy spirit from me," your whole being must be that of one in whose heart Jesus lives. With the earnest petition "Uphold me with a free spirit," the purpose must continually be renewed and carried out: "I will teach transgressors thy ways."

This at least must be your effort and your prayer. When, in the spirit of this psalm, you say, "*Then* will I teach," you may also surely add, "Sinners shall be converted unto thee." If your teaching of others is the fruit of indwelling grace, it cannot remain unblessed. Walk daily in fellowship with Jesus and seek daily the anointing of His Spirit, and "sinners shall be converted."

Observe especially that this confidence must be nourished and expressed in *prayer*. David did not trust in himself and his power; it was while he was looking up to God in prayer that he uttered that glorious word of faith. And indeed it is no light thing for any suppliant to express such confidence in connection with his work. Yet if you will only utter the words as David did, they are also for you. Following the continuous and repeated prayer for grace in all its varied operations and the habitual surrender of yourself to the service of the Lord, with your eye fixed on this God who has shown to you His effectual grace, this hope is not too much to cherish: "I will teach . . . and sinners shall be converted." And if at the redemption as a present fact, a continually renewed and ever-fresh exercise of fellowship with the God of redemption. Whoever does not know God in this way cannot make Him known with power to others. David felt this. How could the murderer of Uriah, stained with the guilt of shedding blood, be able to bring life to others while he is still bound to give an account of the blood of Uriah?

Thus it is impossible for me rightly to teach others, if I do not know God aright myself. And that man does not know God aright who does not know Him as the God of forgiveness. Moreover, this knowledge cannot be living and real if it is not continually renewed from heaven by the Holy Spirit. Every time that, in accordance with my purpose of teaching transgressors and my hope that sinners will be converted, I am prepared to give my testimony, it must be with the prayer, ever expressed anew, "Deliver me, . . . O God, thou God of my salvation; and my tongue shall sing aloud of thy righteousness."

When one considers the words of this petition closely, these thoughts will be found to be still more fully confirmed. Let us reflect on the word *deliver* used in this prayer: "*Deliver* me from bloodguiltiness." This is a term that appears here for the first time in this psalm. It is commonly used, not so much of setting free from sin as of deliverance from enemies that pursue and oppress us. It is so used, for example, in the prayer "Deliver us from the evil one"; and it is from this point of view that David now contemplates his sins. He believes that God has forgiven him and that he has also been washed from his sins. But sometimes there are occasions in the life of the believer when sins that have long since been forgiven rise up again and pursue and overtake the soul. God has forgiven them, but he that committed them cannot forget them and stands in dread of a new outbreak of their violence. The great enemy of souls then makes use of these times of oppression and of these sins to cast the soul down utterly to the dust. For this there is but one remedy. God alone can deliver us from the heavy sense of guilt. But He *can* do it. He can give us such a view of the completeness of His forgiveness and grace that we will be thoroughly delivered from our enemies and know assuredly that sin will have no more dominion over us. He can make us understand the full significance of the glorious words of the New Testament: "He was manifested to take away our sins," in order that we may have "no more conscience of sins" (1 John 3:5; Heb. 10:2). Through the Holy Spirit, God causes us to know the redemption of the Lord Jesus so fully that in it we have the full answer to the petition "Deliver me from bloodguiltiness, O God, thou God of my salvation." And then the enjoyment of such a complete deliverance becomes the urgent impulse to sing aloud of His righteousness. Friend, if you do not yet know if you can celebrate God's praise, come and experience this blessing. Through the Holy Spirit let the glory of deliverance by God become a matter of living knowledge in your heart. Your mouth will then open of itself to celebrate the praise of this God.

The same idea is found in the very name by which David here designates God: "O God, thou God of my salvation." It is because he is the God of *my salvation* that I feel the joyful impulse to praise Him. The personal relation or communion between God and men and the living assurance and experience of it are indispensable for this end. They are all-sufficient to stir me up to make Him known. And if anyone desires to know how he will be able to call God by this name, let him learn it from David. In the beginning of the psalm, he was not yet prepared to use the possessive pronoun. He had several times addressed the Lord as "God," but not yet as "my God." Under the power of continued prayer, however, as well as the constantly renewed plea for grace, his faith is strengthened, and the Spirit of God has given him courage to draw close to God: "Thou art the God of my salvation." So it will be with you also. If with every sin, old or new, you cast yourself before Him, pleading for an experience of the fullness of His grace—forgiveness, renewal, and complete redemption—courage will be given in the midst of your

28

**"And my tongue shall sing aloud
of thy righteousness" (v. 14b).**

Once again, after the petition comes the promise. One who has experienced grace does not selfishly long merely for personal enjoyment or safety, but puts himself out to honor God the Giver and to be a blessing to others who have need of grace. The renewed experience of fellowship with God, as the God of his salvation, will of itself bear the glorious fruit of praise to God: "Deliver me from blood-guiltiness, O God, thou God of my salvation; and my tongue shall sing aloud of thy righteousness."

The words of this promise are significant and instructive. Observe, first of all, the main theme of this joyful celebration: the righteousness of God. It is as if this psalm of grace and redemption could not end without this most glorious theme, in which the work of God in connection with our redemption is presented. The Holy Spirit uses this theme of *the righteousness of God* to indicate to us as well the origin, the way, and the fruit of our redemption. It embraces in one word an *attribute* of God that is glorified in our redemption, the *gift* with which we are endued, and the *operation* and revelation of this redemption in our life. For the person who is yearning to be saved, or for those who have recently been converted, the word *grace* has a most charming sound and appears to be the most attractive and encouraging. The growing knowledge of grace will always bring the ransomed soul to the righteousness of God, as that in which the love of God has its foundation and in which the believer thus also seeks his stability. And therefore to the first promise to teach transgressors God's ways, these words are added, namely, the resolve especially to proclaim also His righteousness. Let us endeavor to understand what this means.

It indicates, first of all, the attribute of God that moves and guides Him in bestowing grace. Grace in the forgiveness of our unrighteousness is not given at the expense of the righteousness of God. No, grace reigns through righteousness; it is from the righteousness of God that grace derives its power. So John writes, "If we confess our sins, he is faithful and just [or, *righteous*] to forgive us our sins" (1 John 1:9). Paul also says that God is righteous when He justifies the ungodly (Rom. 3:26; cf. 4:5). Hence it is that in the psalms and prophecies the righteousness of God is frequently mentioned as that which His people especially celebrate and rejoice in. Some have not been able to understand this and imagine that in these passages the word *righteousness* must be understood as synonymous with goodness. But this is not the case. The righteousness of God, the disposition in Him by which He always does what is right, is the foundation of His throne—also of His throne of grace. Believers have from the beginning been led by the Spirit to understand that the only way by which the unrighteous can be redeemed and become righteous must be that God, the only righteous One, communicates his righteousness to them.

In addition, then, the phrase "thy righteousness" comes to mean the righteousness that is granted to the sinner in God's gracious sentence of acquittal. David had prayed, "Wash me, and I shall be whiter than snow."

That cleanness can be maintained only in the possession of the righteousness of God. The New Testament makes it plain how this can be. In the Mediator, the man Christ Jesus, the righteousness of God is brought near to us. By His obedience and suffering He has brought in an ever-lasting righteousness; and just as by the sin of the first Adam death reigned over all people, so also by this one righteousness of the second Adam grace comes on all who adhere to Him, to justification. And as from Abraham onward faith is reckoned for righteousness, so through all succeeding periods the grace of God that justifies the ungodly has been the hope and the joy of His people. "In the LORD shall all the seed of Israel be justified, and shall glory" (Isa. 45:25).

Then, further, this declaration of David also signifies the effect of the grace of God. The sentence of acquittal by which God justifies the sinner and the righteousness of Christ in which he shares become in him a power of God for sanctification. They are in him the seed of a new life of righteousness. "He that doeth righteousness is righteous, even as he is righteous" (1 John 3:7). Grace reigns through righteousness *to live*. Grace renews the soul after the likeness and the spirit of the righteous One, and the righteousness of God in Christ, first imputed by faith, becomes the new nature in which God's children walk. "If ye know that he is righteous, ye know that every one also that doeth righteousness is born of him." (1 John 2:29).

This is, according to the New Testament, the full significance of "the righteousness of God." And it was of this that David said, "My tongue shall sing aloud of thy righteousness." He saw such glory in it and the revelation of it was for him so delightful and worthy of admiration that he wanted not only to speak of it but also to celebrate its value and worth. He gloried in it as something that had now become his. He praised God for it *joyfully*. This was not a burden laid on him, a mere fulfillment of duty, but something that was his delight; he would speak of it with joy and gladness.

29

"O Lord, open thou my lips; and my mouth shall show forth thy praise" (v. 15).

Once again the promise to celebrate God's praise is repeated, preceded, however, by the prayer that grace itself will give strength for the fulfillment of it. We have already seen that one who has the full and living experience of God's salvation will praise God, just as this tribute is an impossibility without the experience. We see here further, however, that this is also a gift that must be asked from God in prayer. It will then certainly be obtained.

This petition reminds us of the natural reluctance and inability of man to speak of God and to witness to His grace. The experience of almost every believer may serve as a confirmation of this truth. How much there is that keeps one silent, even when he enjoys the grace of God and is eagerly desirous to work for Him. At one time, for instance, it is the fear of man that makes one hesitant in the face of possible mockery and contempt. At another time it is unbelief that, causing one to have a sense of his own unfitness or remember how often the most earnest endeavors are fruitless, takes away all courage and delight in the work. Then, again, there is that hidden self-interest that makes one find an excuse in the needs of his own soul. And yet, once more, there is that show of humility by which one is afraid of doing injury to God's name by confessing Him now, and then presently becoming disloyal and unfaithful, and by which one also learns to say that more can often be done by silence than by speech. Alas! many believers could tell us of a time when they desired to work for the Lord, of months and years spent in wishing and longing, of brief endeavors and swift disappointments, until the shut lips became fixed into a habit, and the conscience, by all sorts of excuses, had brought itself into a state of entire passivity. Would that they had only understood what the true middle way is between sinful silence and precipitate and fruitless speech. Would that they had but understood that, along with the forgiveness of sins and the renewal of life, *grace will also give the opening of the lips,* and that the continued prayer "Have mercy upon me, O God, . . . open thou my lips" will obtain a sure and blessed hearing.

This prayer, then, recorded here by the Spirit of God, assures us that the Lord can and will open the lips. He who sincerely desires to believe that has only to reflect on what is recorded in the Word of God on this point. Read the history of Moses and let the wonderful arguments by which God showed him His power to give him a speaking mouth sink deep into your soul (Exod. 4:10-12). Everyone who will humbly and earnestly listen to the divine words of encouragement will be strengthened in this confidence. Read also the story of the calling of Jeremiah (Jer. 1:7-9) and of the other prophets and see how fully He presents the power to speak as one of His gifts. Consider the promises of the Old Testament about the gift of the Spirit and observe how it is coupled with the power to speak. Mark also the predictions of the Lord Jesus concerning witnessing for Him as the fruit of the gift of the Spirit (John 15:26-27; Acts 1:8). Remember how, on the day of Pentecost, the first manifestation of the power of the exalted Christ filled the mouths of the believers with God's praise, and you will understand what a high place, what a divine certitude, is attached to the opening of the lips as a gift of grace—a gift that truly belongs to us. *God can give it.* He has done so for thousands. God will give it; it is necessary for the accomplishment of His glorious work of grace. *God will give it.* His promises are faithful. "Lord, open my lips" is a prayer we have as much right to pray as this one: "Have mercy upon me, O God." The one is heard as certainly as the other.

David's prayer teaches us the way to obtain this gift. Whenever we mention a speaking mouth, many think of natural gifts, and if one does not have it, he imagines that all that has been said has no application to his case. He will try to serve God in other ways. He will thank God with his money, his influence, his example. This is all good, but it will not serve to liberate anyone from the holy obligation of fulfilling his glorious calling to bring to God also the sacrifice of the lips. It was one of the tokens of the coming of the kingdom of God that not only did the blind see but also the dumb spoke and praised God. The grace of God not only takes the darkness from the eyes so that a person may know Him, but it also opens the mouth so that he may praise Him. Not only are many unclean spirits cast out but also the demon that was dumb. To all the disciples there was given, along with the Holy Spirit, the mouth to praise God. In heaven there are no dumb people; every tongue there praises God. And the Christian in whom the loosened, liberated tongue is not heard is defective. He is lacking in one of the most glorious capabilities of the new man. There is no question here as to whether you have a natural gift for speaking; many who speak little and poorly receive from grace the capacity for achieving great results with that small and feeble gift. It is not beauty of language, it is power of life and spirit that the blessing depends on. Only let your desire to become partaker of this grace also become stronger in the realization of your solemn obligation to praise God and make Him known. Only let every experience of infirmity and inability urge you anew to confidence in the power and promise of God. Out of such a desire and confidence pray, "Lord, open thou my lips; and my mouth shall show forth Thy praise"; and the prayer will be answered. This course may indeed cost you much conflict and perseverance. This rich petition is not learned in one day and the riches of grace are not exhausted in one day, yet he that has the will shall obtain the blessing. Therefore, every time we use the prayer "Have mercy upon me, O God," let it also be with us a fixed rule, a holy habit, to add the petition "Lord, open thou my lips; and my mouth shall show forth thy praise."

30

**"For thou desirest not sacrifice, else would I give it:
Thou delightest not in burnt offering" (v. 16).**

In the joy of deliverance and thanksgiving, David has
surrendered himself to God. Henceforth he will live only
to honor and to praise God. He nevertheless feels how
little it is that he can do, and the question arises within
him whether there may still be something more that the
Lord might possibly desire and receive from him. He
thinks of sacrifices. Might he not, by multiplying these,
accomplish a work that would be acceptable to the Lord?
No, as soon as the question arises, it becomes clear to him
that God has neither delight nor pleasure in sacrifices.

The clearness with which David feels and expresses this
is one of the deep spiritual lessons of this psalm. In "the
hidden part" God taught him wisdom. Sin has become
better known to him than ever before in the deep spiritual
misery it entails. Grace has become known to him in its
high spiritual power. He experienced what the wonderful
work of God in forgiveness and renewal was. He learned to
understand what the symbolical sprinklings and washings
of the Old Testament indicated: how God Himself washes

and purifies the soul. And now along with this spiritual insight into sin and redemption, the Spirit has also revealed to him the spirituality of the life of thankfulness and shown how insufficient the service of external sacrifices would be. Under the old covenant there were two kinds of sacrifices: sin offerings and guilt offerings for atonement, and thank offerings and burnt offerings to represent dedication to God. The discovery of the depths of sin has caused him to feel the need of something more than an external atonement by means of a sin offering, namely, an effectual and divine atonement. Now also he understands that the power of such an atonement enables him to carry out more than a mere external thank offering—that is, an inward and spiritual dedication.

This interrelationship between divine truths will always be seen. The deeper the acknowledgment of sin, the higher the apprehension of a divine supernatural grace, of the divinity of the Redeemer, and of the working of the Spirit, and the more spiritual also the insight into the glory of that new life that grace enables us to live.

In all these respects this psalm is a prophecy of the grace of the New Testament. It is always just in this utterance, "Thou desirest not sacrifice," that the difference between the Old and New Testaments lies. Under the old covenant and according to the law, man must always give God something for taking away sin. In the gospel, on the other hand, God brings to man and gives him what can atone for sin. Under the old covenant man must bring sacrifices to God in the hope that He may receive them. Under the new, God comes to man with a sacrifice, in order that he may receive it and be blessed by it. This is the meaning of the word of the prophet, repeated by the Lord Jesus when He said to the Pharisees, "Go ye and learn what that meaneth, I will have mercy, and not sacrifice" (Matt. 9:13). Not to require and bring sacrifices—for that was the characteristic of the old covenant—but to show and receive mercy is the glory of the new covenant. And thus one who would fully enjoy the salvation of the gospel must above all try to understand the statement "Thou desirest not sacrifice."

This word reminds us of the freedom of God's grace as a source of blessing. The spirit of law-righteousness and work-righteousness is so natural to us that we are always inclined to deal with God as "hard and austere," One who makes heavy demands on us. Would that we could abandon this tendency. God is a God who does not demand but gives, and gives freely; and the secret of fellowship with Him is always to look to Him as a God from whom one may ask and expect everything. He delights in mercy, and not in sacrifice.

That is true of the first grace of forgiveness. How long did you imagine that there was something for you to do in order to become prepared for grace and that there was something you had to bring and offer in order to be acceptable to God? And when faith became plain to you in its simplicity as the reception of what *God had done for you and offered to you,* your response was "Is that all? Is salvation so near, and so easy to find?" Then you learned to understand what David meant by saying, "Thou desirest not sacrifices."

The same thing is true of the higher grace of sanctification. Holiness is not something that we must accomplish. Holiness is only in God, and we become holy only as He makes us share in His holiness. Christ has been given to us for justification, but just as truly for sanctification. One who rightly understands that truth enjoys the salvation of the life of grace as a continuous appropriation and reception of the fullness that is in Christ. He knows now that the life of salvation is not a severe and continued sacrifice, but a glorious experience of what the grace of God in its power and riches works in him. Obedience is better, something higher, than sacrifice: this deeply significant truth lays bare to us the secret of the true service of God. Not what man does or brings, though it is also apparently the performance of the law, but the childlike disposition of loving subjection, is the true fulfilling of the law. If the chief thought suggested by the service of God was once the earnestness, the difficulty, the self-sacrifice involved in it, he who believes eventually comes to the discovery of the joy and the power of the life prepared for him through the compassion of God in Christ. His service of God becomes a service in the joy of love. Love speaks of no sacrifices. Others may indeed glory in the sacrifices that love brings, but love itself does not reckon them sacrifices. To one who loves, they are a necessity, a delight; they are its life.

A disposition like this, which has already acknowledged the gracious attitude of God toward us, also discerns the application to our fellow-men of the statement "I will have mercy, and not sacrifice." It knows how to meet with the fallen in the compassion and tenderness of love, not with the hard requirements and sentences of the law. It understands the secret of the love through which transgressors will learn God's ways and sinners will be converted to Him. "Thou desirest not sacrifice" is the gospel of personal comfort, which in turn is joyfully proclaimed to others.

spirit will, for the believer, always be a token of grace. God may, according to His promise, forget sin; the believer never forgets it. The sense of what it means to be a sinner is not superficial and transitory. It is not something that is very easily effaced. No, for the maintenance and the enjoyment of the right relationship and the right kind of fellowship between the Lord and His redeemed, a person should always continue to be aware of who he is and how much he is indebted to grace. It is just as the Lord said to redeemed Israel, "I will establish my covenant with thee; and thou shalt know that I am the LORD: that thou mayest remember, and be confounded, and never open thy mouth any more because of thy shame, when I have forgiven thee all that thou hast done, saith the Lord God" (Ezek. 16:62-63). It is not only the law and the sense of guilt, but especially the power of grace and forgiving love that will be the means by which the soul will more and more, as time goes on, be humbled and bruised before God. Often the most glorious proof of the goodness of God will suddenly overwhelm the believer and make him remain contrite in the consciousness of his own unworthiness.

This verse also teaches us the delight God has in this spiritual attitude. God has no delight in sacrifice, no pleasure in the mere worth of the greatest external offerings that may be brought to Him. His sacrifice is a broken spirit. It is on the inner self, the hidden person within, that He looks. It is in spirit and in truth that He is to be worshiped. The sacrifice that He desires is a living spiritual sacrifice. And if the one who is seeking salvation, or has already found grace, feels that he has so little to bring to the Lord of what He may reasonably require—nothing of the love, the zeal, the cordial self-surrender, the fervent thanksgiving, which He desires—at such a crisis this verse offers immense comfort: "A broken and a contrite heart, O God, thou wilt not despise." It reminds him that the Lord never finds so much delight in anything as in that feeling of poverty and failure that bows down the soul. This attitude makes the heart capable of receiving and duly appreciating the wonderful grace of God. It teaches one to look away from himself and seek everything in God alone and to give glory to God alone. To such a believer God bows down with inexpressible tenderness and delight to fulfill gloriously for him the manifold promises of His Word. Read the great words of Isaiah on this point (Isa. 57:15; 66:1) and realize that there is no place in the whole world in which the holy God, when He stoops from His glory, will so readily and so certainly set up His throne as in *the contrite spirit*. This is why He devotes so much work to the accomplishment of this bruising of the heart in His children. By the law and the sense of guilt, by the experience of sin and helplessness, by many kinds of adversities and oppressions, by the operations of the Spirit and the revelations of grace—by all this and very much more—He prepares His own for bringing to Him the sacrifice that is acknowledged with the token of His good pleasure.

This verse further teaches us to understand how it is precisely in the broken heart and the contrite spirit that the freedom and joy of the life of grace will be chiefly manifested. This indeed appears a contradiction. It is a contradiction for nature, but certainly not for grace. God's thoughts are not like our thoughts, and the more we by the Spirit appropriate and reduce to practice His thoughts and His Word, the more we will experience how wonderfully our deep misery and God's great grace are wedded to one another, so that His life can be fully revealed only in our death, His power in our weakness, His comfort in our sorrow, His help in our weakness, His healing in our oppression, and His love in our contrition. And we will also experience that the more we die to ourselves and yield ourselves willingly to the discipline of the Spirit, by which our spirit will continually and increasingly be broken so that all of its own hope and power will be taken away, the more we will have the consciousness of God's good pleasure and the experience of His nearness to the broken in heart will become our portion.

If you are moved to pray, "Have mercy upon me, O

32

**"Do good in thy good pleasure unto Zion: build thou
the walls of Jerusalem" (v. 18).**

The psalmist had begun with a prayer for grace for himself. He cannot stop with this, however. The blessed experience of what grace is, as this had been made clear to
him in this prayer, makes him think not only of the transgressors, whom he is now to teach, but also of all who are
partakers with him of this grace, namely, the people of
God. For these also he pours out his heart; he can never
forget the city of God. This is both one of the essential
elements of true prayer and a principal characteristic of
the one who truly prays. The true supplicant is also an
intercessor. Would that we could give good heed to the
important lesson that these last words of the psalm teach
us.

In the first place, the true intercessors for the church of
God are those who have first learned to pray for themselves. Personal need is the school in which true intercessors are brought up. It is in the confession of personal sins,
in the conflict for the assurance of a personal share in
God's grace, that the secret of believing intercession is

learned. There are always many who, in the church and the prayer meeting, plead together for themselves and others and yet know but little of personal dealing with God in the prayer "Cleanse me from my sin." These still know little of true prayer. The sinner must first of all feel as if he were the only one God is concerned with. He must learn to deal with God for himself alone. Then he will learn to understand the grace of God and will know how to plead for this blessing in behalf of the people and the city of the Lord. He then obtains not only courage to speak of God to his fellow-men but also delight in the work; he feels, too, that he has power to speak and plead with God in behalf of his fellow-men.

Those who have thus learned to pray for themselves become intercessors of their own accord. Grace is not self-seeking. The love of God shed abroad in the heart generates love to God's people and church. This was true in the ancient people of the LORD. Think, for example, of the prayers of Ezra and Daniel (Ezra 9, Neh. 9, Dan. 9) and of the way in which the converted Saul of Tarsus bore the congregations of God on his heart. It is on this account that such suppliants are called "watchmen on the walls of Jerusalem" (Isa. 62:6). It is a part of the wonderful honor the grace of God bestows that God makes us fellow workers with Him, and that He uses us in awakening, not only men, but also Himself. He is prepared to take counsel with us and, at our urgent request, He will bestow blessing. Hence it will always be seen that, as soon as there are many in a congregation who in their own experience, learn to understand the grace of God as exhibited in this psalm, the prayer meeting will soon give evidence of the fact in the growing use of the petition "Do good . . . unto Zion."

However, it is not merely the experience of the grace of God in the deliverance from personal sin that moves people to intercessory prayer. There is still something more. David felt himself to be one with the people and, fearing that his sin might possibly prove injurious to the city as a whole, he prayed that these hurtful consequences would be averted. And thus it is with every true suppliant. Aware of the terrible power of sin to carry infection and desolation far beyond the sphere in which it had its origin, the intercessor pleads with the Lord to turn aside the dreaded evil and, notwithstanding his sin, to do good to Zion according to His good pleasure.

"Do good in thy good pleasure unto Zion." It is to God's good pleasure in Zion that intercessors appeal when they ask Him to do good to her. As in the prayer for grace the psalmist appeals to God's lovingkindness and the greatness of His compassion, so here also he turns to God's good pleasure in His people. He does not have to stir up God to show favor, nor does he have to awaken dispositions in God that are not already in existence. No, it is what he knows God to be that gives him power and courage to pray. We should never forget this. Our strongest argument in prayer is the being and the heart of God. The more we are aware of what God has revealed to us concerning His feelings toward His people, and of His purposes and promises, the more we will feel the power to pray. The good pleasure of God toward Zion will be the ground of our hope, the measure of our expectations, and the strength of our assurance of faith. If our souls were only more fully possessed by this conviction, how thoroughly we would feel ourselves aroused by the wonderful thought that God in His good pleasure listens to our poor prayers and will act according to them, and we would pray more earnestly, "Do good . . . unto Zion."

Faith in God's great comprehensive goodness is expressed in the words "Build thou the walls of Jerusalem." That petition includes *building up,* where the walls were not yet completed; *rebuilding,* where they had been broken down by hostile attacks; and *building out,* where they had become too narrow for the growing number of inhabitants. It includes prayer for the spiritual growth and progress of the congregation of the Lord, for the maintenance of God's authority and truth over against the hostile powers of unbelief and the world, and for the extension of the kingdom of God by the ingathering of those who do not as yet know Him.

He who really knows the grace of God and has tried to understand what His plan and good pleasure are with respect to the city He had prepared for His habitation will certainly feel how suitable and necessary this prayer is in our time. How little does Zion, the city of God, the dwelling place of the Most High, exhibit the splendor of the new Jerusalem that John saw descend from heaven (Rev. 21:10). In the midst of severe toil and conflict and much disappointment and numberless hindrances, living stones are being brought in, and the walls slowly rise. There is need of the earnest and urgent prayer, "Build thou the walls of Jerusalem." If you have learned to taste something of the grace of God as expressed in this psalm, make this prayer also your own. In view of the declining life of the people of God and their failure in powerful growth in grace, in view of the growing fury of the attacks of unbelief and worldliness, and in view of the needs of millions who do not yet know the Lord, I urge you, let the grace shown to you rouse you to pray this prayer persistently: "Do good in thy good pleasure unto Zion; build thou the walls of Jerusalem."

God, and the good pleasure of God toward her be made manifest, He would again take delight in the sacrifices of righteousness.

Very important lessons are taught us here. We see, first of all, how the worth of our religion depends wholly on our relation to God. The very same psalm that says, "Thou desirest not sacrifice" says later, "Then shalt Thou be pleased with the sacrifices of righteousness." In the interval between these two statements, a momentous change has taken place. Sin having been atoned for, the good pleasure of God now rests on Zion, and her sacrifices are acceptable to Him. No longer brought to take away unrighteousness or to work out self-righteousness, but as a symbol of the self-dedication and thanksgiving of a justified people—as "sacrifices of righteousness," God can really be pleased with them. This teaches us something of utmost importance in our fellowship with God; namely, that the value of all our works is defined by our relationship to God. If we are not yet reconciled to God, if we have not yet received the atonement and forgiveness of sins in Christ, then our best works cannot be well-pleasing to God. If, on the other hand, we have become the children of God, and the relationship between Him and us is as it should be, then He takes delight in our service and our works, and they are acceptable to Him. Hence it is said, in the words of David, "Thou desirest not sacrifices," but also again, "Thou shalt be pleased with sacrifices"; just as in the words of Paul, we read first, "not of works," but then again as pointedly, "created unto good works" (Eph. 2:9,10). The very same works that, before faith, are worthy to be rejected, are, after faith, and in virtue of it, an acceptable service to God.

Thus we learn further that in all our religion the great question ought to be whether the Lord takes pleasure in it, or whether our work is well-pleasing to Him. That Cain presented a sacrifice availed him little; God did not look favorably on his sacrifice. It matters little that we are earnest and zealous in religion. The great question is whether He takes delight in us and our sacrifice.

It is not how we pray and what we do that can bring us blessing, but the fact that God accepts our praying and our doing and sends an answer to it. Many are content when they think they have done their best to serve God as a matter of duty. With a living faith it is not so. One who truly believes will not merely set the wood in order and slay the victim, but will long for the fire from heaven to consume the sacrifice. He longs to have a token for good, the light of God's countenance, a proof that the sacrifice is well-pleasing and acceptable. He is not merely afraid of a self-willed religion and not merely seeks to serve God with all earnestness in the way ordained by Him, but he desires to know on every occasion that God takes delight in his sacrifices. And by the secret and blessed exercise of fellowship with the High Priest in heaven, which the witness of the Holy Spirit maintains in living interaction with our spirit, this is really bestowed on the one with such faith. The tender-hearted believer may know that God is pleased with his sacrifice.

David's prayer teaches us still further that when God thus takes delight in the sacrifices of righteousness, His people also will take delight in them. "*Then* shalt Thou be pleased . . . then shall they offer bullocks." Yes, it may be easily conceived that nothing will more powerfully incite one to a joyful and abounding service than the blessed certainty that God has delight in it. Many learn by experience to testify that what discourages them in seeking the Lord is that they did not know whether this search was acceptable, because they had no indication that God took delight in it. On the other hand, when we know that God does delight in our effort and that every sacrifice is a joy to Him, how our heart becomes fired and strengthened for duty, and the sacrifice itself becomes a joy and a delight. Yes, the secret of true religion, of a joyful self-surrender and an entire obedience, is the joy of the assurance that God delights in our sacrifices. "*Then will we* offer bullocks on Thy altar."